Get Wise!™
MASTERING Grammar SKILLS

Don't Use No Double Negatives!

by Mandie L. Rosenberg

THOMSON
PETERSON'S

Australia • Canada • Mexico • Singapore • Spain • United Kingdom • United States

THOMSON
PETERSON'S

About The Thomson Corporation and Peterson's

With revenues of US$7.2 billion, The Thomson Corporation (www.thomson.com) is a leading global provider of integrated information solutions for business, education, and professional customers. Its Learning businesses and brands (www.thomsonlearning.com) serve the needs of individuals, learning institutions, and corporations with products and services for both traditional and distributed learning.

Peterson's, part of The Thomson Corporation, is one of the nation's most respected providers of lifelong learning online resources, software, reference guides, and books. The Education Supersite[SM] at www.petersons.com—the Internet's most heavily traveled education resource—has searchable databases and interactive tools for contacting U.S.-accredited institutions and programs. In addition, Peterson's serves more than 105 million education consumers annually.

For more information, contact Peterson's, 2000 Lenox Drive, Lawrenceville, NJ 08648; 800-338-3282; or find us on the World Wide Web at www.petersons.com/about.

COPYRIGHT © 2002 Peterson's, a division of Thomson Learning, Inc. Thomson Learning™ is a trademark used herein under license.

Get Wise!™ is a trademark of Peterson's, a division of Thomson Learning, Inc.

ALL RIGHTS RESERVED. No part of this work covered by the copyright herein may be reproduced or used in any form or by any means—graphic, electronic, or mechanical, including photocopying, recording, taping, Web distribution, or information storage and retrieval systems—without the prior written permission of the publisher.

For permission to use material from this text or product, contact us by
Phone: 800-730-2214
Fax: 800-730-2215
Web: www.thomsonrights.com

ISBN: 0-7689-1077-3

Printed in Canada

10 9 8 7 6 5 4 3 2 1   04 03 02

Acknowledgments

For my husband, Harvey—There really are *so many roads,* I love traveling them with you.

For my sister, Jamie—You're the best friend I ever had or ever will have—thank you!

For my parents, Howard and Susan—It's amazing what unconditional love and guidance will do. You're the best! (And your grammar is impeccable.)

And for Samson (my pooch)—You're the snuggliest!

To Heather McCarron and Farah Pedley, my partners in crime—whoops!—I mean partners in editing—it's been great growing up here with you.

To Wallie Walker-Hammond—for all that coffee (and advice!)

And to Laurie Barnett, your editing and guidance have been so valuable. Thank you.

Contents

Introduction   **1**
So, Why Do I Need Good Grammar?   1
If I Were a Rich Man   2
Have We Confused You Yet?   3
How to Use This Book   5

Chapter 1: The Simple Stuff or...
    Those Boring Basics   **7**
Nouns   10
Adjectives   21
Verbs   29
Voice and Mood   40
Adverbs (Even Verbs Have Modifiers)   46

Chapter 2: The Slightly Less Basic
    Stuff   **53**
Pronouns   55
Conjunctions   81
Prepositions   86

Chapter 3: Grammar Glamour   **93**
The Fully Dressed Sentence   95
Word Order   100
Let's Be Direct (or Indirect)   101
Articles   104
Clauses That Bite!   108
Appositives and Interjections   111
Contractions: The What, the Why, and the How   116

Get Wise! Mastering Grammar Skills   www.petersons.com

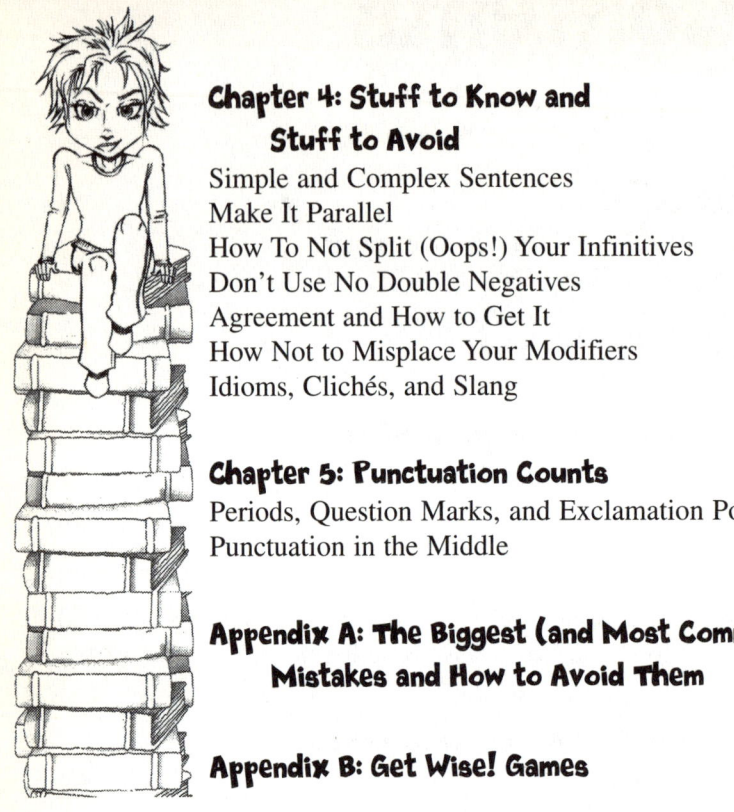

Chapter 4: Stuff to Know and Stuff to Avoid — 119
Simple and Complex Sentences — 121
Make It Parallel — 126
How To Not Split (Oops!) Your Infinitives — 132
Don't Use No Double Negatives — 136
Agreement and How to Get It — 138
How Not to Misplace Your Modifiers — 142
Idioms, Clichés, and Slang — 146

Chapter 5: Punctuation Counts — 155
Periods, Question Marks, and Exclamation Points — 157
Punctuation in the Middle — 160

Appendix A: The Biggest (and Most Common) Mistakes and How to Avoid Them — 189

Appendix B: Get Wise! Games — 197

SO, WHY *DO* I NEED GOOD GRAMMAR?

"D'oh! English! Who needs that? I'm never going to England."

—Homer J. Simpson

Contrary to the thoughts of the esteemed Homer J. Simpson, you *do* need these skills, both to speak and write well in English. Quite simply, a well-spoken person goes further in life. The way you speak affects the way people perceive you, and the way you speak is most probably reflected in your writing. If you speak well, you can write well. (Really, you can!)

Hey, there are tons of accomplished people who don't use good grammar, like, um...well...

Get Wise! Mastering Grammar Skills — www.petersons.com

2 . Introduction

See that, Chi? You can't even think of anyone. Think about newscasters and politicians and the characters on your favorite TV show. Can you think of a cast member on "Friends" who doesn't speak well? No? Neither can we.

IF I WERE A RICH MAN

Huh? What is *that*? If I were a rich man? That's a weird intro to a grammar book.

And how come it's not "If I *was* a rich man"? Isn't that the correct *computation*, or something like that?

Well, first of all, it's not correct *conjugation* because of *condition contrary to fact*, which is one of those crazy grammar rules that deals with the subjunctive tense (which you probably know about from your foreign language classes).

Conjugation is what you do to verbs.
Computation **is what you do in math, and what's pretty sweet about this book is...there's no math.**

What's condition contrary to fact? You'll have to read the book to find out.

www.petersons.com   Get Wise! Mastering Grammar Skills

Introduction . 3

HAVE WE CONFUSED YOU YET?

Good. Now maybe you'll sit up and take notice of the fact that—gasp!—there are things about grammar you don't know. Really. Even after all these years, sitting in English class after English class, you don't know everything. Some of you have spent too much time sleeping through class, passing notes, and not paying attention (you know who you are).

Well, it's time to pay attention to grammar, the oft-forgotten subject. We know many of you may think grammar is boring, but these are things you need to know. When you finish this book, come back to this section. At that point, you can tell *us* what condition contrary to fact is. Want us to tell you now? Tough. You'll just have to read through the book and learn it.

Have we convinced you of the importance of good ol' boring grammar yet? No? Keep reading.

We hope that, after reading this book, you will have achieved two things:

1. The ability to recognize the different parts of speech and to use them for good—not evil!

2. The ability to use your ears to discern correct and incorrect grammar.

But ya' know what? We suspect that grammar is important to you right now (you *are* still reading this), due to that everlasting student question...

Get Wise! Mastering Grammar Skills   www.petersons.com

4 . Introduction

Will This Be on the Test?

Good question. YES! How can we say yes when you haven't even told us *what* test? That's easy. Grammar will be tested (directly or indirectly) on *every* test you might be thinking about taking. Let's look at some of the most common tests for high school students, the SAT and the ACT Assessment.

My teacher always says, "You shouldn't just pay attention to the stuff that's going to be on the test; you should absorb every bit of knowledge you can."
Whatever!

SAT

The verbal section of the SAT I may seem daunting to some students, but it doesn't have to be. The verbal section covers analogies, sentence completions, and reading comprehension. Good grammatical skills will be an invaluable tool on the verbal section—especially reading comprehension. This book will give you the skills you need to feel comfortable with these sections and improve your score.

ACT Assessment

Grammar may be even more important on the ACT Assessment, which explicitly tests usage and mechanics, rhetorical skills, and reading comprehension. Again, your grammatical knowledge will be your friend on this test.

Remember, the SAT II: Subject Tests and the AP exams that require essays will also require good grammar.

HOW TO USE THIS BOOK

This is a book you should work through from beginning to end. We'll begin with the simple stuff and move gradually into more complex stuff. There will be fun games or quizzes after each lesson to make sure you're really paying attention. Even if you think you know all you need to know about a certain concept, humor us and read it anyway. You can never have too much knowledge!

At the end of the book, you'll find Appendix A, which lists the most common grammar mistakes—and we'll tell you how to avoid them. Appendix B has a few more games to help you practice your skills in a fun way. (Yes, you can have fun and learn—even with grammar!)

Enjoy the journey!

chapter 1

The Simple Stuff or...Those Boring Basics

In this chapter, we're going to tell you everything you ever wanted to know and more about nouns, adjectives, verbs, and adverbs (which are the "basics" of the English language). But, before we go into the basics, here are two vital tools you must use to master the English language. (Trust us, they really *will* help you.)

8. The Simple Stuff... or Those Boring Basics

1. The Dictionary (It's not just for definitions.)

Yuck! Who uses the dictionary? Except for my dumb brother. He's at Harvard, now.

Besides definitions, there is another important piece of information that can be found in the dictionary, and that is the *part of speech*. The part of speech tells you the *function* of a word—whether it is a noun, adjective, or adverb. The part of speech is listed at the very beginning of each definition in the dictionary. For example:

yucky \\'yə-kē \ *adj.* Offensive, distasteful.

The abbreviation *adj.* appears after the phonetic spelling of the word and stands for *adjective. Yucky* is an adjective; it describes a noun.

If you're not sure of the word's part of speech, LOOK IT UP! Reference books like dictionaries are for just that—reference. And looking up things in the dictionary will also help you become comfortable researching information, and that's a skill you'll need a lot as you go through high school and college—and, in fact, possibly for the rest of your life.

The Simple Stuff . . . or Those Boring Basics . 9

2. Your Ear

> I hate my ears. They stick out. What the heck do they have to do with grammar?

"My ears?" you ask. What about them?

Not your ears. Your **ear**. Your ear is your greatest ally. Your "ear" is your ability to recognize things that sound right. It is one of the most important tools you will use to achieve good grammatical skills. You have been listening to others speak your whole life, maybe you even read a lot, and your ear has been tuned over the years to recognize things that "sound funny."

Using the dictionary and your ear will help you with the simple stuff—nouns, adjectives, verbs, and adverbs, which are the building blocks of the English language. How so? Well, think of nouns, adjectives, verbs, and adverbs as blocks of different colors and shapes. When you use those blocks to make a castle (or whatever else you'd build with blocks!), the more varied your blocks, the more attractive your building. And without the building blocks, you can't build anything at all! So, building blocks are important, and you **should not** skip this section because, hey, they're building blocks, and, hey, you've got to get them right! We'll try to be quick, and we're going to do the best we can to amuse you along the way. Promise!

So, with all of this in mind, let's begin at the beginning: with nouns.

10 · The Simple Stuff ... or Those Boring Basics

NOUNS

A noun is a person, place, thing, or idea. That's simple, isn't it? Nouns give names to things. Nouns are what you *call* things. How would we communicate without them? Imagine what the world would be like without names for things.

> There would be a whole lot of pointing and grunting at things, I think. Kind of like the conversations my boyfriend has with his buddies.

That's right, Chi, pointing and making random sounds is all we'd have without nouns. And that's how things were before words were "invented." But slowly, the grunts developed into specific grunts for specific things, and before humankind knew it, those grunts and sounds turned into *words*. If you only communicated with nouns, you'd sound pretty weird, but without nouns, you can't communicate at all...which is why we're beginning with the simple subject of nouns.

But not even the most basic part of speech, the noun, is totally simple.

> You know, one thing I've learned is that *nothing* is ever simple, which is really annoying. But, it means you have to pay attention to some things, even if they seem boring. (By the way, the boring stuff's usually on the test.)

The Simple Stuff... or Those Boring Basics . 11

There are many different *types* of nouns. For instance, a noun can be *singular* or *plural*. Whether a noun is singular or plural is very important in sentence structure, and we'll get more into that as we move through the book. Nouns can also be *common* or *proper* and *abstract* or *concrete*. Let's go through all the different types of nouns.

Singular and Plural Nouns

There are rules to help you make singular nouns plural, but as with many rules in the English language, there are exceptions to the rules.

Most nouns can be made plural by simply adding *s* or *es* to the end of the word. Add just an *s* to a noun where the *s* joins smoothly in sound with the word. Some examples are:

> book → book**s**
>
> friend → friend**s**
>
> jellybean → jellybean**s**

All of these words sound "smooth" when you just add the *s,* so you know you don't have to add *es.*

But what about words that don't sound "smooth" with just an *s* tacked on to the end? Those kinds of words end with letters such as *sh, ch, x,* or *z* and take an *es* to become plural. Some examples are:

> grouch → grouch**es**
>
> dervish → dervish**es**
>
> quiz → quizz**es**

Get Wise! Mastering Grammar Skills www.petersons.com

12 . The Simple Stuff ... or Those Boring Basics

Exceptions, exceptions... some words that end in *z* like *quiz* require an additional *z* before you add *es*. Of course, making a verb plural wouldn't be purely simple; otherwise, you wouldn't be telling us about it. Oh well...seems like exceptions are the rule in English!

Indeed, Chi, exceptions in English *are* often the rule. And another exception to making nouns plural concerns words that end in *f* or *fe*. In general, for almost all nouns ending in *f*, replace the *f* with *v* and then add *es*. Some examples are:

knife → kni**ves**

life → li**ves**

And some words do not change at all. Their plural form is the same as their singular form, like *moose*.

The moose **was** standing in the middle of the road. (singular)

But, since the word *moose* can be singular *or* plural, you could also say:

The moose **were** standing in the middle of the road. (plural)

Okay, so how do we, like, *remember* these exceptions? Aren't there any tricks?

www.petersons.com   Get Wise! Mastering Grammar Skills

The Simple Stuff... or Those Boring Basics . 13

Well, sometimes little rhymes can help you remember stuff. Try this one for making words that end in *f* and *fe* plural:

f and *fe* become *v*

my *life,* our *lives* are good as can be!

> **Next time, please warn me if you're going to break into song. What's truly annoying is that now I can't get it out of my head!**

Good! Silly or not, if you can't get the rhyme out of your head, then you'll never forget it!

Be *Wise* about Your Ys

Poor *y*. It's such an outcast letter. It's not a vowel, but sometimes it acts like one. And it has its own rules, so some people don't like it. But we beg you—don't hate the letter *y*. It never did anything to you…and we'll make the rules for *y* easy for you to understand.

Okay. So what *do* you do with words that end in *y*?

When a *vowel* is the letter that comes before the *y* at the end of the word, simply add an *s*:

The **joy** of life → The **joys** of life.

The **boy** ate 100 hot dogs.
→ The **boys** ate 100 hot dogs.

When a consonant (any letter that's not a vowel) comes before the *y* at the end of the word, replace the *y* with an *i* and add *es*.

14 . The Simple Stuff . . . or Those Boring Basics

A **city** is a great place to find museums.
→ **Cities** are great places to find museums.

Learning grammar should be your first **priority**.
→ Learning grammar should be one of your first **priorities**.

Remember, spell-checker can only help you if you're using a computer.

To sum it up, here's how to be *wise* about your Ys:

A   E   I   O   U
There's nothing more for you to do!
Just add an *s*.
There's no finesse.

But if you have a

T   K   S   L   P
or any other consonant that you can see,
replace that *Y*
with your friendly *I*
and add *ES*.

You'll be certain to pass the test!

Help me, help me, help me, please!
The authors have some terrible disease!
They must be nuts.
They're silly indeed.
And you've got 200 more pages to read!

www.petersons.com   Get Wise! Mastering Grammar Skills

The Simple Stuff . . . or Those Boring Basics • 15

Get Wise!

Circle the nouns in the sentences and write the correct plural forms on the line provided below each sentence. (We won't deal with making the rest of the sentence match the plural form of the verb right now; we'll wait until we review verbs—so don't worry.)

1. A blue <u>elephant</u> was eating cream <u>cheese</u> in the <u>refrigerator</u>.
   elephants, cheese, refrigerators.

2. The <u>concert</u> was awesome.
   concerts

3. A compact <u>disc</u> is cool, but a <u>minidisk</u> is cooler.
   discs, minidisks

4. I'd rather have a <u>Corvette</u> than a <u>Porsche</u>.
   Corvettes, Porsches

5. A <u>knife</u> is a useful <u>tool</u>.
   knife, tools

6. My <u>family</u> is so strange that I won't even go to a <u>movie</u> with them.
   families, movies

Get Wise! Mastering Grammar Skills   www.petersons.com

16 . The Simple Stuff . . . or Those Boring Basics

How Wise?

1. A blue elephant was eating cream cheese in the refrigerator.

elephant → elephants, cheese → cheese, refrigerator → refrigerators

2. The concert was awesome.

concert → concerts

3. A compact disc is cool, but a minidisk is cooler.

disc → discs, minidisk → minidisks

4. I'd rather have a Corvette than a Porsche.

Corvette → Corvettes, Porsche → Porsches

5. A knife is a useful tool.

knife → knives, tool → tools

6. My family is so strange I won't even go to a movie with them.

family → families, movie → movies

Common and Proper Nouns

Nouns can either be common or proper. *Common* nouns refer to ordinary objects with general names, such as:

book

paper

pencil

lipstick

Note that common nouns are not capitalized. *Proper* nouns refer to the (duh!) proper names of things. People's names are proper nouns, as are the names of countries, states, and brand names (like Nike). Proper nouns are always capitalized. Here are some examples:

Chi

Africa

Brillo

New Jersey

18 . The Simple Stuff . . . or Those Boring Basics

Concrete and Abstract Nouns

Concrete nouns are nouns we can "touch," such as:

apple

notebook

CD

PlayStation

Get it concrete! Abstract nouns are, obviously, abstract. *Abstract* nouns can be ideas, such as:

freedom

imagination

love

awe

These words are most definitely nouns, but you can't "touch" them.

The Simple Stuff... or Those Boring Basics

Get Wise!

Circle the nouns in the following paragraph and indicate if they are common or proper and whether they are concrete or abstract. Do not get fancy and circle pronouns; we haven't gotten there yet.

Okay. So, I go to (school) [CN,C] and when I get to (Mrs.) [PN] (Hammond's) [PN] class, I find out I have a pop (quiz!) [CN,C]

How much does that stink? I mean, I'm like totally unprepared! I don't even pay (attention) [CN,C] in that (class); [CN,C] usually I do my (nails) [CN,C] or (something). [CN,C] And (Mrs. Hammond) [PN] says, "(Jamie,) [PN] someday you'll learn to be prepared." Who needs (tests) [CN,C] anyway? (School) [CN,C] is too rigid—we should be (free) [A,CN] to do what we want. (Kids) [CN,C] know more than the (teachers) [CN,C] anyway, right?

20 The Simple Stuff... or Those Boring Basics

How Wise?

The circled words are the nouns, the type appears next to them in brackets. Common nouns are concrete unless otherwise indicated. (NOTE: The word "I" is a pronoun, but it is always treated as proper and capitalized.)

Okay. So, I go to (school) [common noun], and when I get to (Mrs. Hammond's) [proper noun] class, I find out I have a pop (quiz)! [common noun] Unbelievable! How much does that stink? I mean, I'm like totally unprepared! I don't even pay (attention) [common noun] in that (class) [common noun]; usually I do my (nails) [common noun] or (something) [common noun]. And (Mrs. Hammond) [proper noun] says, "(Jamie) [proper noun], someday you'll learn to be prepared." Who needs (tests) [common noun] anyway? (School) [common noun] is too rigid—we should be (free) [abstract/common

The Simple Stuff ... or Those Boring Basics . 21

noun] to do what we want. (Kids) [common noun] know more than the (teachers) [common noun] anyway, right?

And now, it's time for those wonderful, adaptable, and descriptive adjectives!

> **How exciting . . . I think this author needs to get a life.**

ADJECTIVES

Adjectives give sentences their flavor. You know, adjectives dress up our words a little. Adjectives *describe* nouns. It's that simple. We've already discussed how hard (impossible) verbal communication would be without nouns. Without adjectives, communication would still go on—but it would be mighty boring and oh so plain! Adjectives can take a plain old noun and make it come to life.

I saw sneakers in a mall.

How can we make that sentence more descriptive?

I saw the **coolest, sweetest** sneakers in a **huge, busy** mall.

See? The second sentence is more interesting than the first because it gives you more *information*—it gives you a much more descriptive *picture* of what the sentence is "saying." But remember, an adjective can do many different things, all while remaining an adjective. What kinds of things? Read on.

Get Wise! Mastering Grammar Skills   *www.petersons.com*

22 • The Simple Stuff... or Those Boring Basics

> Adjectives can be used to *compare* things. Like, Jen has *cool* boots, but Susan's are *cooler*. And Brooke has the *coolest* boots of all. (I'm, like, *so* jealous of Brooke's boots!)

Adjectives can also be used to *quantify* (in other words, to *count*) things, either in concrete numbers (such as: first, second, third) or in ideas (like *cool, cooler, coolest*).

Adjectives can be *positive, comparative, superlative,* or *absolute*. "Great," you're probably thinking, "another grammar point that isn't simple." But don't worry. We'll go through all these things, and you'll see that *adjectives are easy to use*. They really don't change much, no matter how you use them, and they are the most adaptable words in the English language.

Positive Adjectives

These adjectives simply describe the nouns. And, just to make your life more confusing, it is not necessarily a *positive* description. Let's take a look:

Soccer practice was **awful** last night.

"South Park" is a **good** show.

Comparative Adjectives

Adjectives used in the *comparative* way illustrate the *differences* between two things. And, notice in the following example that an adjective *can* consist of two words:

The Simple Stuff... or Those Boring Basics . 23

Last night, soccer practice was **more awful** than the night before.

Here, soccer practice is being *compared* to *another* soccer practice, unlike the "positive" sentence above, which restricts *awful* to just one practice using the word *more*.)

"South Park" is a **better** show than "West Wing."

Here, as above, "South Park" is being compared to *another* show, "West Wing," unlike the "positive" sentence above, which says that " 'South Park' is a *good* show," but does not compare it to any other particular show.

Superlative Adjectives

Superlative has the word *super* in it. This should help you remember that a superlative adjective states that something is *the best* (or *the worst*). You know, like, "Austin Powers is the *super* coolest, and Mini-me is the *super* evilist."

Great tip, Chi—even though *evilist* is not a real word, it gets your point across pretty well! And if you take it a step further, you can remember that *super* is in the word *superior,* which means "better than anything else."

Get Wise! Mastering Grammar Skills   www.petersons.com

24 . The Simple Stuff ... or Those Boring Basics

So, what exactly have we learned? Let's look at some examples using actual words (not *evilist*). The superlatives *most* and *best* in the following sentences indicate that the thing being described is, well, *super*.

> This is the **most exciting** book I've ever read. (I have never read a better book, so the superlative **most exciting** is used.)

> The theater in New York City is the **best** in the world.

(Note: Superlatives are often linked with prepositional phrases, such as *in the world*. These are phrases that begin with prepositions.*)

A Note about Bad, Worse, and Worst (and Other Annoying Exceptions to Adjective Form)

1. Bad → Worse → Worst

2. Bad → Badder → Baddest

Which one of the above is correct? If you picked number 2, we've got a problem (but a correctable one).

You probably know that most adjectives become comparative by simply adding *-er* or *-est* to the end of the adjective (think: *green, greener, greenest*.) But we would like to remind you of the exceptions, such as *bad, worse, worst,* so that you always remember to think before changing the ending of an adjective willy-nilly. Some more examples are:

> good → better → best
>
> little → less (or lesser) → least
>
> many → more → most

---

*We'll talk more about prepositions in Chapter 2.

The Simple Stuff... or Those Boring Basics · 25

> Remember guys, don't confuse slang with proper English. You know, like "He's the *baddest* kid in the neighborhood." It's actually more cool—or is that cooler?—to speak correctly with your friends. It'll become a habit.

It's definitely *cooler* to speak correctly. Thanks, Chi, we're glad you agree.

Absolute Adjectives

These adjectives describe something that is just that: absolute. Absolute words are what they are. Unlike other adjectives, where you can be *sort of* messy or *kind of* pretty or *very* boring, these adjectives stand on their own. An example of an absolute adjective is *vertical*. Something cannot be slightly vertical, or kind of vertical—vertical is vertical. It means straight up and down. (If something is "not quite vertical," then it's **not** *vertical;* it's something else, slanted. Here are some other examples of absolute adjectives:

dead

You're either dead or you're not. At least, I hope!

26 . The Simple Stuff ... or Those Boring Basics

Well, that depends. There's been some debate on whether our math teacher is dead or not. But one thing's for sure—he's *really* boring!

unique

You're either unique or you're not.

square

Something is either a square or it's not.

awesome

Nothing is *kind* of awesome, since awesome actually means something that inspires reverence and wonder. Something either inspires this or it doesn't.

Hey, *awesome* is my favorite word, so I don't misuse it. I save it for my most mind-bending experiences. Last night I saw the incredibly awesome new Blink 182 video—Whoops! I take it back—I saw the incredible new Blink 182 video.

www.petersons.com   *Get Wise! Mastering Grammar Skills*

The Simple Stuff ... or Those Boring Basics . 27

Get Wise!

Circle the adjective(s) in the following sentences and indicate on the lines whether they are positive, comparative, superlative, or absolute.

1. Someone hit a possum, and now it's <u>dead</u>. *absolute*

2. There is nothing <u>better</u> than spending a day at the beach with friends. *comparative*

3. Sharon is the <u>prettiest</u> girl in school; she'll definitely win homecoming queen. *superlative*

4. Western civilization is the <u>most boring</u> subject ever! *superlative*

5. My room is so much <u>cleaner</u> than my brother's; it's not fair that he doesn't get grounded when his room is <u>messy</u>. *comparitive, positive*

6. It's much <u>cooler</u> to be a <u>good</u> student than a slacker. *comparitive, positive*

7. That girl is completely <u>clueless</u>. *absolute*

8. His <u>red</u> Mustang GT is <u>beautiful</u>. *positive*

9. I'm so mad at Adam for that <u>stupid</u> comment he made in gym about my <u>mismatched</u> socks. *positive*

10. Sherri's <u>summer</u> job is <u>fun</u>, but my job is <u>more fun</u>. *positive, comparitive*

Get Wise! Mastering Grammar Skills   www.petersons.com

28 The Simple Stuff... or Those Boring Basics

How Wise?

1. Someone hit a possum, and now it's (dead) **[absolute]**

2. There is nothing (better) **[comparative]** than spending a day at the beach with friends.

3. Sharon is the (prettiest) **[superlative]** girl in school; she'll definitely be homecoming queen.

4. Western civilization is the (most boring) **[superlative]** subject ever!

5. My room is so much (cleaner) **[comparative]** than my brother's; it's not fair that he doesn't get grounded when his room is (messy) **[positive]**

6. It's much (cooler) **[comparative]** to be a (good) **[positive]** student than a slacker

7. That girl is completely (clueless) **[absolute**—you're either clueless or you're not!]

8. His (red) **[positive]** Mustang GT is (beautiful) **[positive]**

9. I'm so mad at Adam for that (stupid) **[positive]** comment he made in gym about my (mismatched) **[positive]** socks.

10. Sherri's (summer) **[positive]** job is (fun,) **[positive]** but my job is (more fun) **[comparative]**

www.petersons.com   Get Wise! Mastering Grammar Skills

VERBS

If there were no verbs in the world, your nouns would sit around all day with nothing to do or nothing to *be! Verbs* are words that express

- ★ *action*
- ★ *occurrence*
- ★ *mode of being.*

Let's take a look:

- ★ A verb of *action* expresses actions, like running, walking, or swimming.

    The girl **swam** quickly away from the shark.

- ★ A verb of *occurrence* expresses that something exists.

    The boy **is here**.

- ★ A *mode-of-being* verb expresses a condition.

    Jessica **is angry** because her parents grounded her.

A verb can be both a word of occurrence and a word of action. Don't worry if you're confused. Read on. It'll become clear. For now, all you have to worry about is how a verb *acts*.

30 . The Simple Stuff ... or Those Boring Basics

Action and Linking Verbs

All verbs can be classified as either *action* (verbs that perform an action) or *linking* (verbs that express a state of being) verbs. Some examples of action verbs are:

run

cry

compete

scream

Linking verbs are slightly different. They do not actually contain a concrete action. Examples of linking verbs are:

are

won't be

am

You may notice that the linking verbs above are really different conjugated tenses of the verb *to be*.

> Simply put, verbs either *do* something or *are* something—unlike my sister, who doesn't *do* anything. Although she really *is* obnoxious (and *complains* all the time).

Action verbs and linking verbs are not too complicated. Try your hand at the following exercise and then we'll move on to the most important issues concerning verbs: tense and agreement with the subject of the sentence. We'll also discuss mood and voice.

www.petersons.com   Get Wise! Mastering Grammar Skills

The Simple Stuff... or Those Boring Basics . 31

Get Wise!

Circle the following verbs and indicate whether they are action verbs or linking verbs.

1. Mr. Smith runs his classes with an iron fist. _action_
2. Julie will be so lucky if she completes the marathon. _linking, action_
3. David walked so far today that we were all surprised. _action, linking_
4. Hey! Don't go in there! _action_
5. Rain ruins my good hair days. _action_

How Wise?

1. Mr. Smith runs [action] his classes with an iron fist.
2. Julie will be [linking] so lucky if she completes [action] the marathon.
3. David walked [action] so far today that we were [linking] all surprised.
4. Hey! Don't go [action] in there!
5. Rain ruins [action] my good hair days.

Get Wise! Mastering Grammar Skills   www.petersons.com

32 • The Simple Stuff... or Those Boring Basics

Tense

> I can define *tense*. It's exactly how I feel when I study grammar! My palms get sweaty, my stomach starts to rumble, and I feel faint and queasy...

Well, that's one definition of *tense!* And we're going to bet you won't feel like that by the time you close this book. The *grammatical* definition of tense has to do with *time*. We use a different *form* of a verb when we use different tenses. The *form* of the verb, quite simply, has to match the *tense*. But what is a tense? Read on for the answer. There are three tenses:

Present, Past, and Future Tense

You hear verbs used in the past, present, and future tense all day. Listen to Chi...

> I *hate* cleaning my room. I *hated* cleaning my room last week, and I *will hate* cleaning my room next week, too.

The Simple Stuff... or Those Boring Basics

What Chi is trying to explain is that verbs have *tense*. This means that **verbs are changed to express a place in time**. The simple tenses are *present*, *past*, and *future*. There are other categories of tenses, such as the *perfect* tense (present perfect, past perfect, and future perfect). But first, let's get the simple tenses down:

★ I *am* writing. (present tense)

★ I *wrote*. (past tense)

★ I *will write*. (future tense)

That was easy. Bet you never thought "tenses" could be so stress-free. Now on to the perfect tense:

The Perfect Tense

Man, those perfect tenses give me a brain sprain. What's so perfect about tenses in the present? Unless you want to give <u>me</u> a cool *present* <u>now</u>, like the new Linkin Park CD, well, that would be cool.

As we have seen, the form of the verb changes when tense is involved. The *perfect* tense is used for actions that have a definite ending. Verbs in the perfect tense can be either *present perfect, past perfect,* or *future perfect.* Let's look at each one.

Present perfect is used when an action ends in the present. This tense is formed as follows:

the verb <u>**has**</u> or <u>**have**</u>

+   a <u>**verb**</u> (any verb!)

+   the ending <u>**ed**</u>

———————————

=   present perfect

Get Wise! Mastering Grammar Skills

34 . The Simple Stuff ... or Those Boring Basics

Let's see how that works. Look at the following sentence:

★ You *have finished* separating 100 bags of Skittles into individual piles by color. (The Skittles have *already* been separated; they are now (in the present) in separate piles by color—although we don't know who would actually do that!)

Let's break that down using the "equation" we gave you:

	the verb **has** or **have**	HAVE
+	a **verb** (any verb!)	FINISH
+	the ending **ed**	ED
=	present perfect	

Now that you know how to use the present perfect, you may have figured out that the *past perfect* tense is used when an action has been *completed in the past*. This tense is formed similarly as follows:

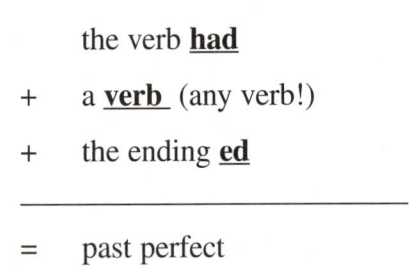

	the verb **had**
+	a **verb** (any verb!)
+	the ending **ed**
=	past perfect

Let's see how this works. Look at the following sentence:

★ Josie *had finished* separating 100 bags of Skittles by color yesterday, so she started to separate bags of M&M's by color. (Here, the separating was completed in the past.)

The Simple Stuff... or Those Boring Basics . 35

Let's break it down using the equation:

	the verb **had**	HAD
+	a **verb** (any verb!)	FINISH
+	the ending **ed**	ED
=	past perfect	

Okay. We've got one more perfect tense to do.

The *future perfect* tense describes an action that is not yet completed but will be completed in the future. Let's look at the equation for the future perfect tense:

	the verb **will** (sometimes **shall**)
+	**have**
+	a **verb** (any verb!)
+	the ending **ed**
=	future perfect

Now, we'll break down the following sentence:

★ Josie *will have finished* separating the bags of Skittles into separate colors by next Tuesday, when she will begin to separate bags of M&M's into colors. (Josie is not yet done separating the Skittles, but she will be in the future.)

36 · The Simple Stuff... or Those Boring Basics

	the verb **will** (sometimes **shall**)	WILL
+	**have**	HAVE
+	a **verb** (any verb!)	FINISH
+	the ending **ed**	ED

= future perfect

> You know, I have understood the perfect tenses. And, I hope I will have understood the perfect tenses when we are tested in the near future. In any case, I had perfected my skills at perfect tenses, so I should be, well, perfect by now!

She's got it! By George, she's got it!

> Okay, that's enough. I got it! Please, no rhymes and no songs!

The Progressive Tense

We're almost done with tense. There's just one more form of tense we need to review. The *progressive tense* is used to indicate an ongoing action (like how a clock is always running) and it works like the perfect tenses. You can use a past, present, or future tense of the verb to make the past, present, and future progressives respectively. So, the progressive is formed like this:

        the verb **to be**

+   a **verb** (any verb!)

+   the ending **ing**

=   the progressive

Let's see how that works. Look at the following sentence:

★ Josie will be finishing the bags of M&Ms by Friday. (Here, the finishing is being completed in the future.)

	the verb **to be**	WILL BE
+	a **verb** (any verb!)	FINISH
+	the ending **ing**	ING
=	future progressive	

Again, the progressive can be either *present progressive, past progressive,* or (you guessed it) *future progressive.*

Hey! If the progressive tense implies an *ongoing* action, how can you have *past* progressive? Isn't that a contradiction or an oxymoron or something? (As opposed to my little sister, who's just a plain old moron!)

38 • The Simple Stuff... or Those Boring Basics

Well, Chi, it may seem like an oxymoron (which is something that is a contradiction, such as jumbo shrimp), but the progressive can describe more than just an ongoing action. It also describes an action that has/had a fixed end point, but that was ongoing for a while. Let's look at some examples in the present, past, and future progressive.

- ★ I **am hating** you right now. (present progressive; the action is ongoing)

- ★ I **was hating** you last week when you got the cool new MP3 player. (past progressive; the "hating" has ended, but was ongoing in the past)

- ★ I **will be hating** you for years to come since you've stolen my girlfriend. (future progressive; the "hating" is going on right now and will continue into the future)

Get Wise!

Rewrite the following sentence in the tenses indicated. Write your answer on the lines provided.

I go to school.

1. past _I went to school._
2. future _I will go to school._
3. present perfect _I have gone to school._
4. past perfect _I had gone to school._
5. future perfect _I will have gone to school._
6. present progressive _I am going to school._

7. past progressive I was going to school.
8. future progressive I will be going to school.

How Wise?

I go to school.

1. past I went to school.
2. future I will go to school.
3. present perfect I have gone to school.
4. past perfect I had gone to school.
5. future perfect I will have gone to school.
6. present progressive I am going to school.
7. past progressive I was going to school.
8. future progressive I will be going to school.

VOICE AND MOOD

> Okay, am I missing something? Verbs are just words, right? How can they have a voice and a mood? That's just what I need, a moody verb! Although . . . that sounds kind of cool.

Voice and *mood* are easy concepts to master, even though they sound somewhat strange.

There are two kinds of voice:

* active voice
* passive voice

And there are three kinds of mood:

* indicative
* imperative
* subjunctive

Active and Passive Voice

The *active voice* of a verb indicates an act that the subject performs.

>Jackie **purchased** squeeze cheese.

In the sentence above, Jackie is performing the action of purchasing. The *active voice* of a verb is usually preferable in writing—it is the most direct way of saying stuff.

The *passive voice* of a verb is used when something is *done to* the subject, as opposed to the subject performing the action.

The Simple Stuff... or Those Boring Basics • 41

Squeeze cheese **was purchased** by Jackie.

The squeeze cheese is the subject of the sentence above. It is *being purchased*. The action is being *done to* the squeeze cheese—the squeeze cheese performs no action.

> Hey! I'll be helpful here! The *active voice* is *strong*; the *passive voice* is *weak*. I usually do stuff to my little brother, like <u>I tease him</u>. My passive little brother, however, <u>is teased by me</u>.

Get Wise!

Each sentence below is written either in the active or passive voice. Decide whether the original sentence is active or passive, and then rewrite the sentence in the opposite form.

1. Janet cooked pasta.
   The pasta was cooked by Janet.

2. The walls were painted by students.
   The students painted the walls.

3. The car was given to me by my parents.
   My parents gave me the car.

4. The dog peed on the fire hydrant.
   The fire hydrant was peed on by the dog.

5. The flowers were arranged by a professional florist.
   The professional florist arranged the flowers.

Get Wise! Mastering Grammar Skills   www.petersons.com

42 The Simple Stuff ... or Those Boring Basics

How Wise?

1. Janet cooked pasta. **[active]** Rewritten as: *The pasta was cooked by Janet.*

2. The walls were painted by students. **[passive]** Rewritten as: *The students painted the walls.*

3. The car was given to me by my parents. **[passive]** Rewritten as: *My parents gave me the car.*

4. The dog peed on the fire hydrant. **[active]** Rewritten as: *The fire hydrant was peed on by the dog.*

5. The flowers were arranged by a professional florist. **[passive]** Rewritten as: *The professional florist arranged the flowers.*

> **I will be spoken to by friends and teachers tomorrow after I'm driven to school by the piece-of-junk car.**

And for fun, try speaking in all passive voice for a day—don't let yourself use active voice. You'll see how frustrating it is when you can't make your point directly, which will help you get how much better the active voice sounds.

Indicative, Imperative, and Subjunctive Moods

As we stated before, verbs can be quite moody. Luckily, unlike people, the moods of verbs are easy to predict and easy to figure out.

The *indicative mood* is used to state a fact, ask a question, or make an exclamation. This is the most commonly used mood in the English language.

- ★ I baked a cake in Home Ec. (*statement of fact*)
- ★ What did you bake in Home Ec? (*question*)
- ★ I baked the most disgusting cake in Home Ec! (*exclamation*)

The *imperative mood* is used to make commands (requests) or give directions. The second person is always used by default in the imperative. The word *you* is implied in all commands.

- ★ Improve your Spanish grade.
- ★ Do your homework.
- ★ Clean your room.
- ★ Please, go get milk.

As I'm sure you've noticed, parents *always* speak in the imperative!

The *subjunctive mood* indicates statements that are **contrary to fact**.

44 . The Simple Stuff ... or Those Boring Basics

> **Hurrah! We're finally here. Now you can find out what *condition contrary to fact* is! I know you've been waiting for this since you read the intro!**

If something is *contrary to fact,* it is not true. But this is what's weird. Of course, instead of being simple and just calling these verbs *untrue,* we call them *subjunctive.* And here's the weird part, if it's subjunctive (or untrue), you conjugate in the third-person plural form. Huh? Yes, it's weird. There's no good reason for it. That's just the way it is—a strange rule, and one you just have to remember. Let's return to the example we used in the Introduction to this book: the line from the song in *Fiddler on the Roof.*

If I were a rich man . . . I wouldn't have to work hard.

Note that we say, "if he *were* rich" instead of "if he *was* rich." It's **not true** that the man is rich, so we conjugate as if *he* were *they,* which is third-person plural. The subjunctive tense most often contains the word *if,* which sets up the contrary condition.

Use *were* for the past subjunctive and *be* for the present subjunctive. Here are some more examples of the subjunctive mood.

★ Megan insisted that *she be permitted* to retake the math test. (**present subjunctive**)

★ If she *were* more attentive, she would not have to retake the test. (**past subjunctive**)

★ Megan's sister said, "If I *were* you, I'd study my butt off and pass the test or Dad'll take your car away!" (***past subjunctive***)

Now you see that verbs are indeed moody, but it's really not that complicated. We'll check out what you've learned, and then we'll move on to the last part of this chapter, *adverbs*.

Get Wise!

Read each sentence below and write whether it is indicative, imperative, or subjunctive in the blank provided.

1. Clean up this mess! _imperative_
2. Are you okay? _indicative_
3. If I were taller, I would be a model. _subjunctive_
4. Unless you give me that, I'll kick your butt. _subjunctive_
5. Run! _imperative_

How Wise?

1. imperative
2. indicative (question)
3. subjunctive
4. subjunctive (remember, the subjunctive is used for untrue *and* hypothetical statements)
5. imperative (Short sentence, huh?)

ADVERBS (EVEN VERBS HAVE MODIFIERS)

We know that nouns have adjectives to modify them. But adjectives are not the only game in town. What do verbs have to modify them? That's right—*adverbs*. Adverbs do lots of things besides modifying verbs. Mainly, adverbs also modify adjectives and other adverbs. But don't panic! We'll teach you about adverbs in no time (and with no pain)!

The most complicated part about adverbs is remembering that they do not modify nouns. Everything else is easy because adverbs act a lot like adjectives. They quantify and compare just like adjectives. But because both adjectives and adverbs modify things, you have to be careful not to get them mixed up.

First, a good thing to remember is that many adverbs end in *ly*, and this is an easy way to identify them.

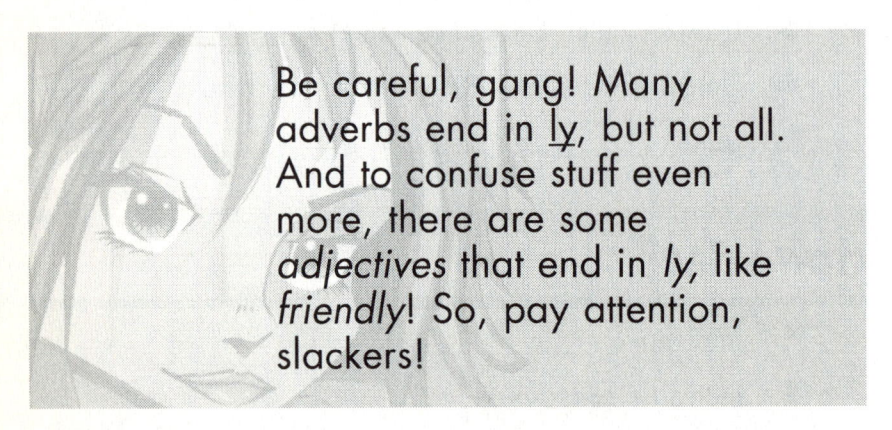

> Be careful, gang! Many adverbs end in <u>ly</u>, but not all. And to confuse stuff even more, there are some *adjectives* that end in *ly*, like *friendly*! So, pay attention, slackers!

Adverbs tell you where, how, when, and how often the action (verb) occurs.

★ The students groaned *loudly* when they got the pop quiz. (How did the students groan? *Loudly*. Here, the verb *groaned* is being modified.)

The Simple Stuff... or Those Boring Basics . 47

★ Amy is *frequently* angry with her boyfriend. (How often is Amy angry with her boyfriend? *Frequently*. Here, the adjective *angry* is being modified.)

★ The students groaned *very* loudly when they got the pop quiz. (How loudly did the students groan? *Very*. Here, the **adverb** *loudly* is being modified.)

Get Wise!

Circle the adverbs in the following paragraph and indicate whether they modify a verb, an adjective, or another adverb.

Pigglywigs are the hottest new thing. Kids are running (wildly) to their local stores, which are (desperately) stocking their shelves and frantically reordering stock. Every kid in America has gone (absolutely) gaga over the (fantastically) green items. Parents are too (rabidly) concerned about this, though. It's just a fad, after all. Why would parents (overly) and (unrealistically) expect kids to derive bad messages from the Pigglywigs? I don't know, but Pigglywigs must be a (really) terrific item.

How Wise?

Pigglywigs are the hottest new thing. Kids are running (wildly) [modifies a verb] to their local stores, which are (desperately) [modifies a verb] stocking their shelves and (frantically) [modifies a verb] reordering stock. Every kid in America has gone (absolutely) gaga over the (fantastically) [modifies an adjective] green items. Parents are (too) [modifies an adverb] (rabidly) [modifies a verb] concerned about this, though. It's just a fad, after all. Why would parents (overly) [modifies a verb] and (unrealistically) [modifies a verb] expect kids to derive bad messages from the Pigglywigs? I don't know, but Pigglywigs must be a (really) [modifies an adjective] terrific item.

Adverbs Quantify and Compare

Just like adjectives, adverbs quantify and compare. The degrees of comparison are the same as those for adjectives: positive, comparative, and superlative.

- ★ James acted *diabolically*. (**positive**)
- ★ James acted *more diabolically* than Mica. (**comparative**)
- ★ James acted the *most diabolically* of all. (**superlative**)

Some Weird Adverbs

There are also some adverbs that are not used for comparison. Similar to absolutes, they are not quantifiable—they can't be "counted." You will just have to know them. Some examples are:

almost   **there**

ever   **too**

never   **very**

It's cool nowadays to say, "I had a *real* good time last night." I hear it all the time. But even I know that grammatically, it's wrong. It should be "really good time." This is the correct way to use the adverb "really."

Special Adverbs

> I never thought there was anything *special* about adverbs, so what are these? Some kind of elitist, snobby word creatures?

There are some adverbs that are so special, they make up their own class. These are:

interrogative adverbs

affirmative adverbs

negative adverbs

This is easier than it sounds. Really. We promise you will recognize all of the words in these categories. You just may not know that they are adverbs. Unfortunately, whoever created the grammatical rules felt it necessary to use these complicated words to describe things.

Interrogative adverbs are the "question" words: how (as in "How much…?"), why, when, and where. Simple, right? Well, not as simple as *affirmative* and *negative* adverbs.

The *negative* adverbs are **no** and **not**. The *affirmative* adverb is **yes**.

★ *No*, I will *not* let you copy my homework.

★ *Yes,* I will let you copy my homework.

Remember that **yes** and **no** are unique adverbs in that they comprise a complete answer to a question in and of themselves.

The Simple Stuff... or Those Boring Basics

Now that you've wrapped up your study of the very basics of English grammar, we'll move on to the next chapter. And just like in math, where you build on the basics, we'll build on your grammar basics and send you well on your way to impeccable grammar skills!

chapter 2

The Slightly Less Basic Stuff

What do you mean by "slightly less basic"? Slightly more yucky?

If the concepts you learned in the first chapter were the *only* concepts you knew, you would lead a life of very robotic sentences comprised only of a noun, verb, adjective, and maybe an adverb.

> Paige ran quickly. Paige was afraid. Paige got away.

54 • The Slightly Less Basic Stuff

These sentences tell you what happened to Paige, but they're not very descriptive and are quite repetitive. But take a look at this:

> Paige ran quickly away from the madman. She was very afraid of him, and she ran until she finally, thank heavens, got away.

The sentences above flow better than the sentences in the first group, and this makes them more interesting. The language is varied and more information is supplied. And by the way, all of the points we'll cover in this chapter are included in the second example:

pronouns

conjunctions

prepositions

By the time we're done, you'll be able to use them all with ease.

PRONOUNS

Before we dive into pronouns, please note: The rules for pronouns can seem complicated, but we're going to make them simple for you. Don't worry if you get confused, because most *adults* can't get these rules right! But we're going to teach you some tricks to make sure you always use them correctly. And that's the most important thing to remember with this book—using the tricks and shortcuts we provide is okay. So, if you just want to use the tricks, that's cool. But we've also included more in-depth review for those of you who are interested. (And even if you're not interested right now, maybe someday you'll need the info—and you'll know just where to get it!)

In any case, soon you will not only amaze your friends and neighbors but also you will be able to correct the grammar of all the adults in your life!

Here's what's nice about pronouns: As they take the place of nouns in a sentence, they follow the same rules. And you've already mastered the rules for nouns in the first chapter. So, you're ahead of the game! But it's not all easy; you do need to learn about the different *types* of pronouns and when to use them.

We're going to discuss six kinds of pronouns:

personal

possessive

reflexive

reciprocal

demonstrative

relative

56 · The Slightly Less Basic Stuff

> I get *personally* insulted and *possessive* when my boyfriend is *demonstrative* toward some other girl, especially when she's a *relative* of mine at a family thing. I know our feelings for each other are *reciprocal*, but maybe I'm being too *reflexive* about this.

That's really clever, Chi! We'll begin with personal pronouns.

Personal Pronouns

> My mom has a personal trainer. She's so lucky. What do I get? A personal pronoun. Great...

Personal pronouns are part of the subject of a sentence, and they can take the place of the person *speaking* (first person), the person being spoken *to* (second person), or the person being spoken *about* (third person). Look at Chi's comment above. She uses two pronouns (in bold):

> My mom has a personal trainer. **She's** so lucky. What do **I** get? A personal pronoun. Great...

Here, Chi uses the third-person pronoun *she* to talk about her mom. Chi uses the first-person pronoun *I* to talk about *herself*, as Chi is the speaker. Personal pronouns can be one of two things: subject pronouns or object pronouns.

The subject pronouns are:
- *I / we* (first person)
- *you / you* (second person)
- *she, he, it / they* (third person)

These are the object pronouns:
- *me / us* (first person)
- *you / you* (second person)
- *her, him, it / them* (third person)

A *subject pronoun* acts as the subject of a sentence and an *object pronoun* acts as the object of the sentence. Object pronouns are **never** the subject of a sentence.

58 . The Slightly Less Basic Stuff

Stupid Quirky Rule

The personal pronouns **you** and **it** do not change in form regardless of their case. Actually, **you** doesn't even change form from singular to plural. (I can't believe I even know this!)

Thanks for the info, Chi. Another silly rule you need to remember is that the pronoun *you* **always** takes the plural form of the verb. This is just one of those rules you'll have to remember. So *don't* ever say:

You is never going to believe this.

because the singular form of the verb *to be* is mistakenly used. This sentence is incorrect (and what most grammarians consider an inexcusable error!). Say instead:

You *are* never going to believe this.

Here, the plural form of the verb *to be* is used correctly with the pronoun *you*.

Some of the most common pronoun confusion occurs with personal pronouns and what case to use. For example, is it "Dora and *I* go shopping" or "Dora and *me* go shopping"?

★ Remember that **subject** pronouns must be part of the **subject** of the sentence; this means that the pronoun "performs" the action. "Dora and I go shopping." Dora and the speaker are performing the action of shopping, so they are the subject of the sentence. You need the *subject pronoun* "I" to replace the *subject* of the sentence.

The Slightly Less Basic Stuff . 59

★ The **object** pronouns always "receive" action. "The store fired Dora and *me*." *Me* is the pronoun in this sentence and is correct, as opposed to "The store fired Dora and *I*," because Dora and the speaker (me) have "received" the action of firing.

A Word to the Wise

Deciding between *Me* and *I*: Here's a way to figure it out that's actually easy. Use your "ear"! If the sentence is:

Danny gave a valentine to Caroline and _____

and you're not sure if you need to use **me** or **I,** remove the word "Caroline" and see if it sounds right. "Danny gave a valentine to *me*." See? You'd never say "Danny gave a valentine to *I*," so *me* must be correct!

This, of course, works with third person as well:

She was laughing at Jessica and **he**.

This is incorrect. "She was laughing at *he*" is also incorrect. But use your own ear and try it. "She was laughing at *him*." That sounds better, right? So, the sentence should read:

She was laughing at Jessica and **him**.

See that? When you use your ear, grammar is easy!

Get Wise! Mastering Grammar Skills

60 . The Slightly Less Basic Stuff

Get Wise!

Fill in the correct personal pronoun as indicated in the parentheses that follow the blank.

1. The pigeon pooped on Craig and _me_. (**first person, singular**)

2. Tommy is so cute, but the prom picture that the photographer took of Angela and _him_ (**third person**) came out horrible!

3. It's your thing, do what _you_ (**second person**) want to do.

4. Amy and _I_ (**first person**) think Erica's hair looks totally fried.

5. _They_ (**third person, plural**) accidentally threw the frog we were supposed to dissect out the window, and it hit the Principal!

How Wise?

1. me
2. him
3. you
4. I
5. They

Possessive Pronouns

Possessive pronouns show possession. Duh! We told you it wasn't that much more complicated. But there are two kinds of possessive pronouns: those that modify nouns and those that are used as personal pronouns.

The possessive pronouns that modify nouns are:

* ★ *my / our* (first person)
* ★ *your / your* (second person)
* ★ *her, hers, his, its / their* (third person)

These pronouns answer the question *Whose?* They work like adjectives because they "define" the noun. Look at the following example for clarification:

> The **orange** cat decided to live with the neighbors.

Here, *orange* is the adjective; it modifies *cat*. Now, if we want to replace the adjective *orange* with a pronoun, we could say:

> **My** cat decided to live with the neighbors.

Here, we replaced the adjective *orange* with the pronoun *my*. *My* modifies *cat*, just like the adjective *orange* modified the word *cat* in the previous sentence.

The possessive pronouns that are used as personal pronouns are:

* ★ *mine / ours* (first person)
* ★ *yours / yours* (second person)
* ★ *her, hers, his, its / theirs* (third person)

62 . The Slightly Less Basic Stuff

These pronouns do not modify nouns, but they are used to show possession. Specifically, they tell you **who** possesses the noun. Here are some examples:

>Those Pumas are **mine**. (Whose shoes are they? **Mine**)

>**Our** science lab ended in disaster. (Whose lab? **Our** lab)

>**Your** boyfriend is a pig! (Whose boyfriend? **Your** boyfriend)

>**Her** taste in clothes is horrendous. (Whose taste? **Her** taste)

Get Wise!

Select the correct pronoun from the choices given in the following sentences.

1. (**my, mine**) _____ Mustang is the coolest car in the senior lot.
2. Don't touch that, or (**your, yours**) _____ fingers will fall off!
3. That ugly uniform is (**their, theirs**) _____, not (**our, ours**) _____.
4. Give that back, it's (**her, hers**) _____!
5. The blame is (**my, mine**) _____, and (**my, mine**) _____ alone.

How Wise?

1. my
2. your
3. theirs, ours
4. hers
5. mine, mine

Stupid Quirky Rule

Possessive pronouns <u>never ever ever</u> take an apostrophe! Ever!

The minivan is their's (**Incorrect**)

The minivan is theirs (**Correct**)

Reflexive and Reciprocal Pronouns

We're going to discuss reflexive and reciprocal pronouns together because they have a characteristic in common: Neither can act as the subject of a sentence.

The reflexive pronouns are:

- ★ myself / ourselves
- ★ yourself / yourselves
- ★ herself, himself, itself / themselves

The reciprocal pronouns are:

- ★ one another
- ★ each other

The terms *reciprocal* and *reflexive* will probably not come up on any standardized test, so don't worry about the terms. But you may have to *use* these pronouns on a test, and you should know how to do so, even if you don't remember the terms.

The Slightly Less Basic Stuff . 65

But sometimes the names of things can help you remember them. For example, you can call reflexive pronouns *mirror* pronouns. This'll help you remember that reflexive pronouns *reflect* the action of the verb back toward the subject like a mirror! We'll call them mirror pronouns from now on to make things easier.

> **My sister looks at *herself* in the mirror all the time! Her *reflection* usually reciprocates her compliments. She's *sooo* vain.**

Mirror pronouns are formed using the suffixes *-self* and *-selves*. When these suffixes are added to personal pronouns, the pronouns become *reflexive*. Let's look at the mirror pronouns again, and then we'll look at some examples:

★ *myself / ourselves* (first person)

★ *yourself / yourselves* (second person)

★ *herself, himself, itself / themselves* (third person)

Here are some examples:

I love **myself** when I say something brilliant.

You should get **yourself** together before the test begins.

He got **himself** arrested after he vandalized the turnip farm.

Get Wise! Mastering Grammar Skills   www.petersons.com

66 . The Slightly Less Basic Stuff

Let's talk about *each other* and *one another.* These are called the *reciprocal* pronouns. Remembering how to use *each other* and *one another* is something that most adults get wrong all the time! Really. It's amazing because the rule is pretty simple. Armed with the rules in the bulleted list below, you can now correct every adult you encounter who uses these pronouns incorrectly. Sure, they'll be annoyed, but that will make it even more fun!

- *Each other* is used when referring to **two** people, **two** things, **two** animals—you get the picture.

   Maya and I helped **each other** do well on the SATs.

- *One another* is used when referring to—you guessed it!—**more than two** things.

   Jessica, Maya, and I helped **one another** do well on the SATs.

Get Wise!

Select the correct reflexive or reciprocal pronoun from the choices given and write your answer in the blank provided. (Yeah, we're giving you choices again. We want you to learn this stuff…we don't want to torture you!) Not every choice will be used.

myself	each other
one another	yourself
himself	herself
itself	ourselves

1. You _____ should know better than anyone else not to do that.

2. The girl and boy assisted _____ in building the sandcastle.

3. Oh, look at that poor, sad Christmas tree all the way in the corner by _____.

4. The members of the drama club really try to help _____ improve their techniques.

5. I can't believe I did this to _____ again.

Get Wise! Mastering Grammar Skills

How Wise?

1. yourself—the pronoun *you* should clue you in
2. each other—there are only **two** people
3. itself—*tree* is third person, so you need the third-person reflexive pronoun
4. one another—there are **more than two** people
5. myself—the pronoun *I* should clue you in

Demonstrative Pronouns

Demonstrative pronouns *demonstrate* stuff—duh again! You can think of them as *pointing* pronouns because they "point to" the thing about which you are talking, and they're easy to remember—there are only two.

The pointing pronouns are:

* this / these
* that / those

This and *these* are used to indicate objects that are close by (either in actual space or in time).

This dress looks awful on me.

The dress is close both physically and in a time sense, since the present-tense verb tells us that the speaker is currently wearing it.

These shoes look awful on me as well.

Same reasoning as above, only *these* is plural.

The Slightly Less Basic Stuff . 69

These authors are driving me nuts with *this* stuff!

The book, and therefore, the authors, are "close" to Chi in space and time, so her use of *these* and *this* is correct.

That and *those* are used to indicate objects that are **not** close by in time or distance.

> **That** is my girlfriend standing at the end of the hall, talking to that other guy!

The girlfriend is not close by; she's at the end of the hall.

> **Those** are your shoes hanging over the phone wire.

The shoes are up in the air and not close to the speaker.

You can also use pointing pronouns as adjectives. When demonstrative pronouns act as adjectives, they look like this:

> **This** lunch is horrendous; what is Lunchlady Doris doing? (Which lunch? **This** lunch)

> **That** boy is a P-I-G pig! (Which boy? **That** boy)

This and *that* are adjectives in the previous sentences. They answer the question *Which?* They describe the *lunch* and the *boy* in the same way that an adjective would. Try it out by substituting an adjective for the pronouns:

> **This** lunch is horrendous; what is Lunchlady Doris doing? (The **greasy** lunch…)
>
> **That** boy is a P-I-G pig! (The **gross** boy…)

Get Wise!

Circle the demonstrative pronouns in the following paragraph. Then, put a line through those that are used incorrectly, and write the correct form above them.

Well, well, well. What have we here? This is just unbelievable! Of all the things I expected to see, those is not one of them! These is the worst time for this to happen. I mean, I saw my paper on her desk across the room, and I was like, "Give me this!" Really, I can't believe she copied my paper, and handed it in to our professor before I handed mine in! Those is the worst day of my life!

72 The Slightly Less Basic Stuff

How Wise?

Well, well, well. What have we here? (This) [correct] is just unbelievable! Of all the things I expected to see, ~~(those)~~ *this* is not one of them! ~~(These)~~ *This* is the worst time for this to happen. I mean, I saw my paper on her desk across the room, and I was like, "Give me ~~(this!)~~ *that*!" Really, I can't believe she stole my paper, and handed it in to our professor before I handed mine in! ~~(Those)~~ *This* is the worst day of my life!

Relative Pronouns

> Oh, please, something that has to do with relatives can't be good. My relatives are nothing but an embarrassment...every last one of them.

Stop freaking out on us, Chi. This is easy, too. We just don't have a cute term to replace *relative*, so you can just memorize what they are from the list that follows:

who

whom

that

which

what

why

where

when

Relative pronouns can do two things. Besides taking the place of a noun, like all pronouns, they also connect two parts of the

74 . The Slightly Less Basic Stuff

sentence. What's nice about the relative pronouns is that they do not change or conjugate to match first, second, or third person. For example:

> I did **what** I was told, so why am I still in trouble? (first person)
>
> You did **what** you were told, so why are you still in trouble? (second person)
>
> She did **what** she was told, so why is she still in trouble? (third person)

The pronoun *what* stays the same in all of the sentences above, even though the speaker changed from first to second to third person.

> **Hey! Relative pronouns are not all simple. What about *who* and *whom*? Can't I just forget about the stupid word *whom*? *Whom* needs it anyway?**

Okay, Chi used *whom* incorrectly. And we also find the whole thing pretty annoying. Unfortunately, the word *whom* does exist, and just about no one knows how to use it correctly, but we're going to teach you how with a never-fail trick:

> If a personal pronoun or a proper noun subject follows the "who" in a sentence, change it to **whom**.

The Slightly Less Basic Stuff . 75

How does this work? Take a look at the following sentence:

> It is Janis Joplin **who** I love more than any other singer of all time.

As we said above, a proper subject ("I" in this case) follows *who*, so change the *who* to *whom:*

> It is Janis Joplin **whom** I love more than any other singer of all time.

As you can see, "I" is the proper pronoun, so the *who* becomes *whom*.

> I don't like that girl **who** he invited to the dance.

Again, the *who* should be *whom* because the *who* is followed by a pronoun:

> I don't like that girl **whom** he invited to the dance.

There is one little catch, though…

The trick *always* works **except** in one case, and that's where the verb **to be** is involved. That means if you see the words *is, are,* or *am,* you need to use **who**. Therefore, the following sentence is correct:

> It is you **who** I love.

Although *who* is followed by the pronoun "I," "is" is also in the sentence, and "is" is a form of *to be*. Stick with "who."

Get Wise! Mastering Grammar Skills   www.petersons.com

76 • The Slightly Less Basic Stuff

Note: For those of you who want to have the technical explanation, here it is…

In the nominative case where *who* becomes the subject, use *who*. Use *whom* for the objective case. And use *whose* for the possessive case. So:

The girl **who** is my lab partner is very weird.

To **whom** am I speaking?

Whose ugly scarf is that?

Stupid Quirky Rules

Different relative pronouns are used for different things. Here are four rules for relative pronouns.

1. *Who* and *whom* (whichever you decide to use after using the trick we just gave you!) are always used for people. They are never used for animals and things. So you wouldn't say:

The dog **who** ate my homework…

A dog is **not** a person. Instead, you'd say:

The dog **that** ate my homework…

However, if you are referring to a pet by name, it is acceptable to use *who:*

> My dog **Samson, who** is very cute, ate my homework.

If *who* and *whom* are used for people, then what do you use for animals and things? Well…

2. *Which* and *that* are used for animals and things. Please note that *which* is never used for people, but *that* can be used for people (although *who* is always preferrable to *that* when referring to people).

> The boy **that** forgot his gym shorts looks funny in those borrowed sweats.

This is okay, since you can use *that* for people.

> The gym, **which** smells rank, is my least favorite place to be.

You can't say, "The gym, **who…**" because *the gym* is not a person; but your friend Jim is!

3. *What* is used for objects and never refers to people or animals.

> She really knows **what** she's doing.

78 . The Slightly Less Basic Stuff

4. *When,* *where,* and *why* refer to time, places, and reasons respectively.

The day will come **when** I'll finally graduate.

This is the first place **where** I feel comfortable.

I don't know **why** we park on driveways and drive on parkways.

Get Wise!

Select a relative pronoun from the choices given to fill in the blanks in the following paragraph. Some of the choices will be used more than once.

---

where   who   that   what
why   which   when

This story is about the huge gross-out in my biology class today. We had to dissect a worm. How gross is _____(1)! And _____(2) person do I get stuck with as a lab partner? Weird Larry! And he was actually excited about dissecting a worm! I mean, he's the only person I know

_____(3) would get excited about something like

_____(4). Anyway, I can't get the moment

_____(5) we cut the worm open out of my mind.

So icky! I didn't want to continue, but I know

_____ (6) happened to Diane when she re-

fused to dissect the worm—she flunked the assign-

ment. I honestly don't know _____(7) we had to

do this project. I can't figure out _____ (8) my

teacher gets these crazy ideas, anyway.

How Wise?

This story is about the huge gross out in my biology class today. We had to dissect a worm. How gross is *that* (1)! And *which* (2) person do I get stuck with as a lab partner? —weird Larry! And he was actually excited about dissecting a worm! I mean, he's the only person I know *who* (3) would get excited about something like *that* (4). Anyway, I can't get the moment *when* (5) we cut the worm open out of my mind. So icky! I didn't want to continue, but I know *what* (6) happened to Diane when she refused to dissect the worm—she flunked the assignment. I honestly don't know *why* (7) we had to do this project. I can't figure out *where* (8) my teacher gets these crazy ideas, anyway.

CONJUNCTIONS

Conjunctions are the words that connect two phrases or words. You know, conjunctions are important words—they bring together other words. What a nice thing to do. Think of conjunctions as **joining** words. That is, they *join* other words together. There are three kinds of conjunctions: *coordinating, correlative,* and *subordinating,* and they act in different ways.

Coordinating Conjunctions

Coordinating conjunctions connect parts of a sentence that are *equal* to one another. The coordinating conjunctions are:

but

and

or

nor

for

yet

so

These conjunctions can either *tie things together* (**and**) or *show differences* (**but, or**).

Farah **and** I go to the store.

Here, the conjunction ties *Farah* and *I* together.

Farah went to the store, **but** I did not go with her.

Here, the conjunction tells us that *I* did something **opposite** from *Farah*.

Correlative Conjunctions

Correlative conjunctions really act like the previous coordinating conjunctions, but there are **two** words—in other words, correlative conjunctions come in *pairs*! The most common correlative conjunctions are:

- either…or
- neither…nor
- both…and

The most important thing to remember about these pairs of conjunctions is that they must always be used in their pairs—you can't mix them:

Incorrect: Neither Trey or Mike is my favorite member of Phish.

This is wrong because we mixed *neither* with *or,* and you have to use *nor* with *neither*.

Correct: **Neither** Angel **nor** Angela could understand why the teacher kept getting their names confused.

Here, the pair *neither/ nor* is used correctly.

Incorrect: **Either** you tell Fred, **nor** I will.

Here, *nor* is incorrect because you can't use *nor* with *either*.

Correct: **Either** you tell Fred, **or** I will.

Here, *either/or* are used correctly together.

Note: Does anyone know *why* you can't mix *either* with *nor* and *neither* with *or*?

We know! Because *either/or* implies a positive, and *neither/nor* implies a negative, and it wouldn't make sense to combine them.

Subordinating Conjunctions

Subordinating conjunctions connect parts of a sentence that are of unequal importance and can't stand alone as a sentence.

Some subordinating conjunctions are:

after	as if	because
before	even if	even though
except that	if	in case
since	unless	until
when	while	wherever

I will paint my dog's toenails pink **after** I give her a bath.

Here, "after I give her a bath" can't be its own sentence, so it gets the subordinating conjunction *after*.

See? Conjunctions aren't really that hard. Try the next exercise and then we'll move on to prepositions.

Get Wise!

Each item below has two sentences. Connect the two sentences using a conjunction. Rewrite the sentences on the lines provided.

1. Peter put gum in Gabbie's hair. She needed peanut butter to get it out.

2. Platform shoes are cool. Brigette twisted her ankle wearing platform shoes.

3. Go to school. Don't go to school.

4. I would have gotten an "A" in chemistry. Mr. Peach hates my guts.

5. Jack went up the hill. Jill went up the hill.

86 • The Slightly Less Basic Stuff

How Wise?

1. Peter put gum in Gabbie's hair, **and** she needed peanut butter to get it out.
2. Platform shoes are cool, **but** Brigette twisted her ankle wearing *them*.
3. *Either* go to school *or* don't go to school.
4. I would have gotten an "A" in chemistry, **except** Mr. Peach hates my guts.
5. Jack *and* Jill went up the hill.

PREPOSITIONS

Prepositions are words that show relationships. They indicate time, location, and direction. *Of, from, under,* and *with* are examples of prepositions.

> Unlike "the cheese" in "The Farmer in the Dell" (remember that childhood rhyme?), prepositions never stand alone.

Prepositions are part of a phrase called a *prepositional phrase*. You don't have to commit the term to memory, but it's important to remember that **prepositions are *always* part of a phrase**. Look at the following example:

She is always **in**.

The Slightly Less Basic Stuff . 87

The phrase above uses the preposition *in*, but there is no phrase to go with *in*. So you end up with an incomplete sentence, because a preposition can't stand alone. Look at the example again with a complete prepositional phrase:

She is always **in the principal's office**.

Here's a great trick Chi's seventh-grade teacher taught her class to help them figure out if a word is a preposition. It's called the **House Test**. Think of a house. The house will be what is called the "object" of the preposition. (You should remember this term, because it will help you remember that prepositions need objects, because as we said above—prepositions never stand alone.)

I slept through everything in that class except this. Imagine that!?

88 . The Slightly Less Basic Stuff

Back to the house. Place a word in relationship to the house:

House 1

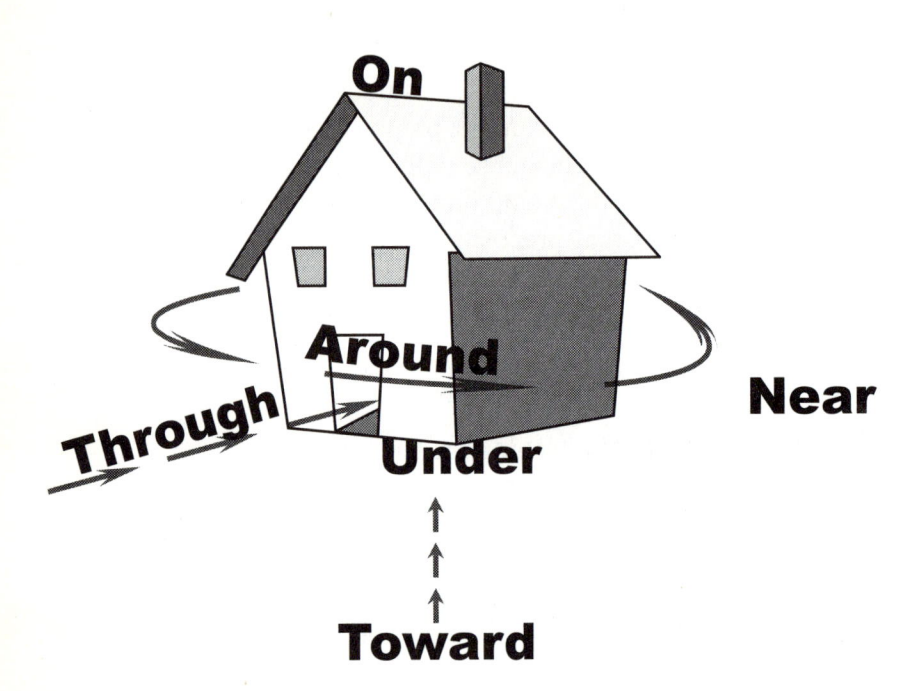

On, Around, Through, Under, Near, Toward (labels on house diagram)

All of these words are prepositions. They all indicate location in relation to the house. And they all make sense. Let's look at how words that are not prepositions work with "the house."

Pink the house. (**Pink** doesn't make sense here, so you know it's not a preposition.)

Bird the house. (Again, **bird** doesn't make sense, so it's not a preposition.)

The Slightly Less Basic Stuff . 89

Identifying prepositions is the hardest thing about them. So remember, *if the word doesn't pass the "house test," it's not a preposition.* Once you can confidently identify them, learning to use them correctly is easy. With that in mind, try the following exercise to make sure you can identify prepositions with ease.

90 . The Slightly Less Basic Stuff

Get Wise!

Here is a list of words and a picture of a house. Write the words where they would belong in relation to the house.

> in   over   under   nearby
> against   beside   off   on

House 2

The Slightly Less Basic Stuff . 91

How Wise?

House 3

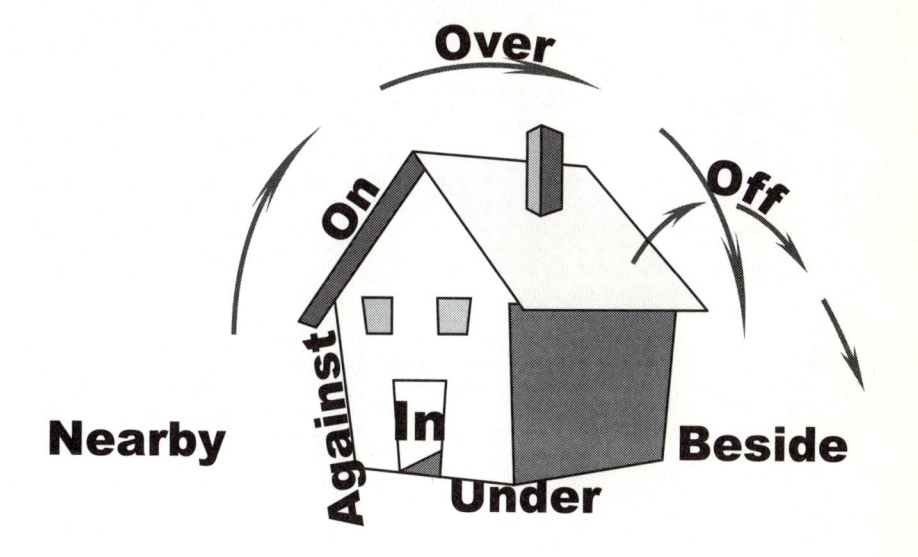

Over

On

Off

Nearby

Against

In

Under

Beside

Get Wise! Mastering Grammar Skills   www.petersons.com

chapter 3

Grammar Glamour

Grammar glamour? How is grammar glamorous? Julia Roberts is what I consider glamorous. You'll have to convince me about this…

We're going to convince you, Chi. Because grammar isn't just about words; it's about language as a whole. And sentences *can* be glamorous, because language can be glamorous. Sentences give form to your words. They allow you to express yourself. Sentences have *style,* like Julia Roberts has style. Think about people who's style you admire.

What's so cool about them? It's not just the individual things they wear or what their hair looks like—it's the *combination* of all those things.

Style is not just about one skirt, or one bracelet, or one pair of shoes. It's about how you put those things together. For a sentence, words are like the individual articles of clothing that are put together to make a sentence (the style).

And there are many kinds of style. That's what makes the English language and grammar so cool. There are endless amounts of sentences you can make. Think about all the sentences you'll say in your entire life—the number is so large it's inconceivable. And that's what's so wonderful about sentences: they're available in an endless supply. You could never ever in your whole life write down every sentence there ever was or is or ever will be.

Wow. This is deep.

It really is deep. We could go on for hours. Think about all the good books you've read, or TV shows or movies you've seen. Books, TV shows, and movies are made up of sentences. And think about how lucky you are to be able to hear the sentences—unlike people long ago who had to watch silent movies. You have the luxury of enjoying all the beautiful sentences and paragraphs and books and movies that talented people (well, most of the time they're talented) write.

And, now that you know how to link up words, grammatically speaking, we'll talk about the sentence itself. The things you learn in this chapter will help you write and speak clearly using all kinds of sentences. You'll be better prepared for tests like the ACT Assessment and the SAT. Like the chapter before this one, you won't have to commit all the terms you learn to memory, as long as you understand the concepts. We will relate each point to specific common grammatical errors, and we'll make sure you know how to get them right. And we'll try, again, to be more interesting than your curmudgeonly old English teacher.

THE FULLY DRESSED SENTENCE

A complete sentence is fully dressed. That means it has the two essential parts of every sentence: a *subject* and a *predicate* (the part with the verb). Without these two parts, your sentence is half dressed? You wouldn't leave your house half dressed, so why should your sentences be half dressed? Think about how embarrassed your sentences would be if they were half naked! What a nightmare!

Believe it or not, many people have trouble with the concept of making sure sentences are fully dressed—wearing pants, if you will. But, aren't you lucky? You learned about using "your ear" as a tool, and your ear should always "tell" you if a sentence is incomplete—when in doubt, read a sentence aloud. But it also helps if you know the facts, so read on.

Tee hee...Half-dressed sentences. You guys actually said something funny. I can't believe it. And I can't stop thinking about a sentence with no pants on!

Get Wise! Mastering Grammar Skills   www.petersons.com

We mentioned the words *subject* and *predicate* earlier. The word **subject** makes sense for what it pertains to—the *subject* of a sentence is what the sentence is about. The word **predicate** is just weird. If you knew Latin or something, you could maybe figure out where this word comes from, but who really cares? The *predicate* tells us what the subject is *doing* or *experiencing—it always includes the verb!* There are really no other words to help you remember these terms without getting confused. You would have to think of something like:

> **predicate** sounds like **predict**, which is a verb, and the verb is in the predicate

But, since you will not likely be tested on exact terms, you can think of the subject as the *shirt* of the outfit that is a sentence, and you can think of the predicate as the *pants*. We'll use the terms interchangeably, but if you find that *shirt* and *pants* are easier for you to remember, mentally replace the words *subject* and *predicate* with *shirt* and *pants* when you see them.

> **Here comes a sentence in boldface; you should probably pay attention to it.**

All complete sentences have a shirt (a subject) and pants (a predicate). A sentence without both of these parts is not a sentence at all. Or, as we said earlier, it would be half dressed.

This is a "sentence" without a predicate:

> The gnarly thing

Not really a sentence, is it? Here's a "sentence" without a subject:

> is the grossest thing I've ever seen.

Also not a sentence. Neither is "also not a sentence." See how important having both parts of a sentence is? Nothing drives teachers more crazy than incomplete sentences (well, perhaps illegible writing). "Is the grossest thing I've ever seen" has two verbs, but it has no *subject*; therefore, you can say it "has no shirt."

> I [subject] run [predicate].

This is a short sentence, but it has both a shirt (**I**) and pants (**run**). These are "simple" subjects and predicates—they have no embellishments and are therefore easy to recognize. But what if there are more than just two words in the sentence?

> The drippy ice cream [subject] dripped all over the cute little boy [predicate].

In this sentence, *ice cream* is the simple subject, and the whole phrase "The drippy ice cream" is a *complete subject*. This means that there are words to modify the simple subject, like a logo modifies a simple shirt. The same holds true for the predicate.

Get Wise!

Choose a subject or a predicate from the list below and match it to the incomplete sentences to make them complete. Write the letter in the blank provided. One choice won't be used, and the choices can begin a sentence, even though they are not capitalized.

1. _____ are called inch worms.
2. _____ An apple a day.
3. _____ your test score yet?
4. _____ Cassidy.
5. _____ are made of marshmallows and sugar.
6. _____ I think you.
7. _____ Britney Spears broke up.

- a. with Justin Timberlake
- b. I think
- c. *Peeps*
- d. look stupid in those pants
- e. have you gotten
- f. is both pretty and smart
- g. green worms
- h. keeps the doctor away

How Wise?

1. __g__ are called inch worms.
2. __h__ An apple a day.
3. __e__ your test score yet?
4. __f__ Cassidy.
5. __c__ are made of marshmallows and sugar.
6. __d__ I think you.
7. __a__ Britney Spears broke up.

WORD ORDER

We just talked about subjects and predicates, so now we'd like to say a quick word on *word order*. Word order is the order in which your words appear, and it is very important. Changing the order of words in a sentence can change its meaning.

> The teacher failed Michelle. (This means the teacher gave Michelle a failing grade.) BUT...
>
> Michelle failed the teacher. (This means Michelle "disappointed" the teacher.)
>
> The Jets scored the winning touchdown over Miami. (The Jets won.) BUT...
>
> Miami scored the winning touchdown over the Jets. (Miami won.)

If you can remember as far back as the beginning of this chapter, think about what would happen if you could count all the sentences there ever were, and then you changed the word order in all of them. You'd have twice as many sentences as before. (Just something to ponder...)

These are simple examples, but they illustrate how important word order is to clear communication. Keep this in mind; it will help you understand the next subject, *direct and indirect objects*.

LET'S BE DIRECT (OR INDIRECT)

Objects go with verbs. They tell us *what* is receiving the action and "to whom" or "for whom" the action is happening. Knowing about direct and indirect objects is important, because it will help ensure that your sentences make grammatical sense.

A **direct object** is the object in the sentence that is having an action performed on it. It answers the questions *Who?* and *What?* Hence, *direct* object.

> I washed the car. (Here, **car** is the direct object. It is receiving the action of "being washed.")

An **indirect object** usually refers to people and answers the questions *For whom?* and *To whom?* It *always comes before the direct object.* There is not always an indirect object in a sentence.

> Andrew gave **me** (indirect object) a **corsage** (direct object). The **corsage** is being given to **me** (which answers the question **To whom?**).

Why are direct and indirect objects important? You may see these terms on an exam, and if you take French or Spanish, you will most definitely run into them. Think of direct and indirect objects as accessories, like earrings or watches, to the shirt and pants of your sentence. Putting together a sentence is like putting together an outfit.

> An outfit's not an outfit without accessories. So if accessories make an outfit better...oohhh...I get it now. I like this clothing analogy!

Get Wise!

Circle the direct objects and underline the indirect objects in the following paragraph.

Family Road Trip

My dad planned a road trip for the family last year. I was not excited. He gave me an MP3 player to bribe me to go. And I'm sorry I did. My brother made me have a headache every day! We went out West. I met a boy at Yellowstone Park. He gave me his phone number. That was cool. I wrote letters to all my friends to keep myself from going crazy. I wrote my cousin a letter, too. I bought my little brother a straw hat in New Mexico when we stopped there. Are you bored with this story, yet? I'm bored with it.

How Wise?

My dad planned a (road trip) [**direct object**] for the family last year. I was not excited. He gave me [**indirect object**] an (MP3 player) [**direct object**] to bribe me to go. And, I'm sorry I did. My brother made me [**indirect object**] have a (headache) [**direct object**] every day! We went out West. I met a (boy) [**direct object**] at Yellowstone Park. He gave me [**indirect object**] his (phone number) [**direct object**]. That was cool. I wrote (letters) [**direct object**] to all my friends to keep myself from going crazy. I wrote my cousin [**indirect object**] a (letter) [**direct object**], too. I bought my little brother [**indirect**

object] a straw (hat) [**direct object**] in New Mexico when we stopped there. Are you bored with this story, yet? I'm bored with it.

ARTICLES

There are three *articles* in the English language.

> So what? There are about 500 articles in the *New York Times* every day!

That's right, there are lots of articles (stories) in the *New York Times*. But we're talking about *grammatical* articles, which are NOT articles *about* grammar. They're *words* that are *called* articles. They are:

the

an

a

And if you think about how many *grammatical* articles appear in each of the articles in the *New York Times*, the number is going to be way, way bigger than 500! Articles seem like such silly little words, but they're so important. And you've got it easy in English grammar, since there are only three articles. English uses the same articles for every gender. In Spanish, there are lots of articles, because they can be feminine or masculine—at least you don't have to worry about that!

Sorry. Where were we? Articles are used before nouns to *define* them, like adjectives define nouns. In fact, for a long time, articles were considered adjectives. Lately, though, they have begun to be treated as a separate thing. But they act like adjectives, and since you mastered adjectives in the first chapter, articles will be easy. (Such small words should never be hard, anyway.)

The is a *definite article.* This means **the** refers to specific people, places, or things and is used with both singular and plural nouns.

> When my class visited **the** White House, Eric mooned a security guard, and we all got kicked out of the tour!

Here, "White House" is a specific thing.

A and **an** are *indefinite articles.* This means they refer to people, places, and things that are NOT specific. They are not used for plural nouns, only singular.

> When my class visited **a** white house, Eric mooned a security guard, and we all got kicked out of the tour!

This is not *the* specific White House but *a* white house—and why would there be a security guard at an ordinary white house, anyway?

See how changing an article can change the meaning of a sentence?

Your "ear" (along with common sense) should tell you which article to use, and most people don't have a problem deciding whether to use **the** or **a/an**. But you'd be surprised how many people have trouble with **a** and **an**.

1. Use **an** when the article comes before words that begin with a vowel *sound.*

    an invitation

    an apple

    an heir (Notice, *h* is not a vowel, but this word begins with a vowel *sound.*)

2. **NEVER** use *an* before a word that begins with a consonant sound. Here's a little pet-peeve of ours, coming from the East Coast:

    He has **an** history with her.

    This is INCORRECT. Some people make the *h* "silent" in words like *history* when they speak. This is wrong. It's not **AN ISTORY**, it's **A HISTORY**.

3. Use **a** when the word after the article begins with a consonant sound.

    a girl

    a loser

    a winner

Get Wise!

Place the correct article—**a, an,** or **the**—in the corresponding blank.

1. She was _____ obnoxious and jealous person.
2. _____ movie *American Pie* was awesome.
3. Do you want to go to _____ movies with me tonight?
4. The signing of _____ Declaration of Independence was _____ historic event.
5. _____ awful thing happened to Dan; he got stuffed in his locker by seniors.

How Wise?

1. She was *an* obnoxious and jealous person.
2. *The* movie *American Pie* was awesome.
3. Do you want to go to *the* movies with me tonight?
4. The signing of *the* Declaration of Independence was *a* historic event.
5. *An* awful thing happened to Dan; he got stuffed in his locker by seniors.

CLAUSES THAT BITE!

There are two kinds of clauses: clauses that **bite** (restrictive) and clauses that **don't** (nonrestrictive). But restrictive and nonrestrictive are awfully big and scary words for an easy topic. Knowing about these kinds of clauses helps you decide whether to use *which* or *that*. Why does that matter? Because adults can never seem to get it right. In fact, we have even heard some grown-ups say, "I use *which* because it *sounds* better." This is flat-out wrong. Using a word incorrectly *never* sounds better. But, once you're done reading this short section, *you'll* be able to correct the adults! Although that may not go over so well...

We'll abandon the fancy terms now. Here's how you decide when to use *which* and when to use *that*.

Both *which* and *that* are pronouns used to *define* something.

Use **which** when the thing you are defining is not essential to the sentence.

> The blue bear, which had been Andy's favorite from the beginning, survived its trip through the washing machine.

Here, the phrase "which had been Andy's favorite from the beginning," is **not essential** to the sentence. In other words, the sentence would still be complete without the nonessential information.

> The blue bear survived its trip through the washing machine.

Here's a neat trick:

You usually need a comma before the word *which*. Think of it this way, "which with a hitch," or "there's a 'c' in which, so that means you need a <u>c</u>omma." And <u>never</u> use a comma before *that*. If you think a comma truly belongs in the sentence, you probably need to use *which* instead of *that*.

Use **that** with phrases that are essential to the sentence.

> The bear that went through the washing machine was his favorite.

Here, the phrase "that went through the washing machine" is essential. It defines "bear." If you took the phrase out of the sentence, you wouldn't know *which* bear. You can also follow the opposite of Chi's tip. Could you put a comma after *bear*? If not, use *that*.

Get Wise!

Instead of a written exercise, listen to your local news this week. Listen to the newscasters use *which* and *that* and apply the rules you just learned. You will be surprised how many times you hear *which* used incorrectly. If you really want to have fun, listen to your teachers. Wouldn't it be kind of cool to correct your favorite one?

APPOSITIVES AND INTERJECTIONS

Appositives

Appositives are easy, easy, easy. An appositive is a group of words surrounded by commas, and it defines a word in a sentence. It's easier to show you appositives than to define them, so look at the following examples:

> Angelo, my best friend, is class president.

Here, "my best friend" defines *Angelo*.

> Erica, a huge snob, does not like my sneakers.

Here, "a huge snob" defines *Erica*.

> **Erica *is* a huge snob, by the way. But she does have good, and I mean really good, taste in clothes. So I'm kinda' bummed that she doesn't like my sneakers.**

Chi's used appositives well there, even though we don't really care about Erica. Here's her comment reprinted with the appositives in italics:

> Erica is a huge snob, **by the way** (this defines the whole first half of the sentence). But she does have good, **and I mean really good** (this defines Erica's taste), taste in clothes. So I'm kinda bummed that she doesn't like my sneakers.

Remember, appositives must **always** be set off with commas. However, if an appositive comes at the end of a sentence instead of in the middle, you will only need **one** comma—the one before the appositive if it ends the sentence.

> My brother plays in a Wiffle Ball league, the *Weekend League.*

Here, the name "Weekend League" defines *what* league.

Appositives are a great way to further accessorize your sentences. They are another tool that can change the pattern of a sentence. They are really useful—they can make your sentences more interesting by combining two short, boring sentences. Look at the following sentences:

> I go to the best high school in the state. Its name is J. Edgar Boring High School.

This would be a smoother and perhaps more elegant sentence if it read:

> I go to the best high school in the state, J. Edgar Boring High School.

The difference between these two examples is subtle. But subtle things like that add to the *style* of a sentence. And, as we discussed in the beginning of this chapter, the infinite number of styles of sentences adds to the flavor of the language.

Interjections

Interjections are words or phrases that express emotion and appear in the middle of a sentence or between sentences. Interjections can be made of real words, like "oh, my!" or "sound" words, like "BAM! SPLAT! OUCH!" **Curse words are interjections**. We hate to say it, but that, more than anything else, will probably help you remember what interjections are. You can punctuate interjections in one of two ways:

1. Use a comma to separate the interjection from the sentence if it does not need to be *really* set off.

   Gee, you really are smart.

2. If the interjection is very strong, set if off with an exclamation point.

   Holy cow! That's incredible!

Here are some more examples of interjections (in bold) using words that *are not* curse words:

Yikes! There's a ghost over there!

Ouch, that hurts!

Oh my gosh! That's the scariest thing I've ever seen.

Get Wise!

Choose the *appositive* or *interjection* from the following list that best completes each sentence below and put it in the corresponding blank with punctuation.

> Wow
>
> Blech
>
> the Eagles
>
> Beth
>
> the cutest boy in school

1. David _____ asked me for my phone number.
2. Kara plays for the state soccer league _____.
3. _____ Having your pants pulled down in gym must be so embarrassing.
4. I hate roaches _____ they really gross me out.
5. My sister _____ tried out for "The Real World."

How Wise?

1. David, *the cutest boy in school,* asked me for my phone number
2. Kara plays for the state soccer league, *the Eagles*.
3. *Wow!* Having your pants pulled down in gym must be so embarrassing.
4. I hate roaches. *Blech!* They really gross me out.
5. My sister, *Beth,* tried out for "The Real World." (Note: This is only correct if Beth is the *only* sister, otherwise, the phrase would be "My sister Beth" with no commas.)

CONTRACTIONS: THE WHAT, THE WHY, AND THE HOW

The What

A contraction is two words (or sometimes a word) that are *contracted* together by removing a letter or letters and replacing it with an apostrophe. The purpose of contractions is to *bring the two words together*. There are common contractions in English. But why did they develop in the English language? Weren't the original two words that make up a contraction good enough?

The Why

Why do we have contractions? Contractions mimic speech. Over time, in common speech, certain words were combined. And let's face it, we just love to make things quicker, faster, shorter. We're not experts in linguistics, but we know that written contractions have been around for a long time. Think of the "Star Spangled Banner":

> O'er the ramparts we marched...

O'er is a contraction, although it's an obsolete one. You probably use other contractions, such as *won't* and *don't*, every day.

> I don't want to practice the piano.

The How

Contractions are a sticky subject. You've probably noticed that this book is littered with them. And you're probably thinking (if you've ever paid attention in English class), "Hey, I thought you were not supposed to use contractions in writing." You're right. In formal writing—any school writing (except creative writing), essay contests, standardized tests—stay away from contractions. However, in creative and informal writing, contractions are okay. They make for a nice, informal, and relaxed tone. That's why we feel okay about using them freely. But we don't use the contraction **ain't** (am not). *Ain't* **is never ever correct to use.**

Which brings us to an interesting question. This won't be on any test, and we don't know the answer. Maybe you can find someone who does? The question is:

Why is **ain't** not an acceptable contraction?
What's different about **ain't**?

We know that, historically, *ain't* was viewed as a kind of low-class word. So, it was snobbishly excluded from proper English speech. But why? Why *ain't*? It never picked on anybody. It's okay to say *aren't* for *are not*, but not to use *ain't* in place of *am not*.

If you can find an answer other than "society said so," we'd love to know. Contact us via our Web site, www.petersons.com, if you find an answer. (Address your commentary to the Editorial Department.)

Anyway, back to the acceptable contractions. Some common contractions are:

cannot → can't
is not → isn't
does not → doesn't
have not → haven't
will not → won't
shall not → shan't
are not → aren't
do not → don't
I am → I'm
I have → I've
could have → could've

should have → should've
would have → would've
might have → might've
she is / she has → she's
he is / he has → he's
it is / it has → it's
that is / that has → that's
what is / what has → what's

Notice that *cannot* becomes *can't,*

with the apostrophe replacing the letters *n* and *o*. But *will not* and *shall not* become *won't* and *shan't* respectively.

You probably use many of the words in the preceding list all the time. And, again, that's okay (we just did it!). But please keep the contractions out of class papers, tests, and formal situations.

Get Wise!

Instead of testing you on contractions on paper, try this: Do not use contractions for a full day. See how hard (and weird) it is. Remember, that is what all of your formal writing should "sound" like.

chapter 4

Stuff to Know and Stuff to Avoid

Now that we've taken you through the basic training camp of grammar (phew!), it's time to go a bit deeper into the woods.

Lions and tigers and bears, oh my!

120 • Stuff to Know and Stuff to Avoid

Well, it's probably more like:

idioms and slang and split infinitives, oh my!

But, these things are not quite so scary. (Although what could really be scarier than lions, tigers, and bears?) Or, at least they won't be so scary by the time you've gone through this book. What they *will* be, unfortunately, is on all those standardized tests we all know and love. (Ha!) But, not to fear…

> *Not to fear?* **What the heck does that mean? It's not grammatically correct, that's for sure!**

Actually, Chi, "not to fear" is an *idiom* and a great example of the kind of stuff we'll teach you in this chapter. We'll also teach you about things like simple and complex sentences and how to avoid some pretty common grammatical errors. And we *will* have tricks for you, and we'll even keep letting Chi make comments—if she's not entertaining *us*, maybe she'll at least entertain herself! And you never know, she may have a trick or two of her own to tell you about.

So, let's get going on our trip into the woods.

SIMPLE AND COMPLEX SENTENCES

> Great! Now we're gonna learn that sentences have *complexes*? I know all about complexes. Every one of my friends has got a complex about something—like hair, weight, popularity. What kind of complex could a sentence have?

Sentences don't *have* complexes! But they can *be* complex. In the last chapter, we learned about putting together a sentence. So, *simple* and *complex* sentences is a really simple subject (no pun intended). You already learned about the *parts* of a sentence. And you learned about how the variety of sentences adds to the *style* of language. Learning about simple and complex sentences will help you add even *more* style to your sentences. Let's simplify. Sentences can be either *simple* or *complex*. And they are what they sound like.

A **simple** sentence can be as short as two words:

I scream.

A simple sentence can even be one word—subjects can be *implied* in commands:

Run!

122 . Stuff to Know and Stuff to Avoid

Complex sentences are…

> **Get ready—more complex. Duh!**

Okay, Chi, when you're right, you're right. Complex sentences have more words and more information than simple sentences.

I scream for ice cream.

Run, or you'll get cooties!

Can you really *outrun* cooties? We're not sure. Anyway, getting back to business:

Q: Why do you need to know about simple sentences?

A: Whether you are writing or speaking, you don't want to use all simple sentences because you will sound boring and robotic.

> I love shopping. I love the mall. There are lots of cool things at the mall. There are lots of cute boys at the mall.

Stuff to Know and Stuff to Avoid . 123

Chi, that's an incredibly robotic passage. You sound like the Terminator would sound if he ever went shopping at the mall—although he did destroy a couple of mall window displays in *T2*.

Q: How can you make that sound more like it is spoken by a human and not a cyborg?

A: You can use *conjunctions* to join simple sentences and make them *complex*. However, when you combine sentences, you will need to get rid of some unnecessary words in order to avoid repeating yourself.

Let's see how that works:

I love "Dawson's Creek." I love "Buffy the Vampire Slayer"

→ I love "Dawsons Creek" **and** "Buffy the Vampire Slayer."

I hate cartoons. I like "South Park," however.

→ I hate cartoons, **but** I like "South Park."

124 • Stuff to Know and Stuff to Avoid

Get Wise!

Each of the following problems has two simple sentences. Use one of the following conjunctions to make the simple sentences one complex sentence and rewrite the sentence on the line provided.

and   but   for   therefore   so

1. I like to study bugs. I will major in bugology in college.
   _____

2. She is a good actress. She fakes crying to get herself out of quizzes all the time.
   _____

3. I love to dance. I will study business in college.
   _____

4. Snorks have a snork. Snorks live under water.
   _____

5. She will go to the Institute of Toenail Study. She is destined to do so.
   _____

How Wise?

1. I like to study bugs, **so** I will major in bugology in college.
2. She is a good actress, **therefore** she fakes crying to get herself out of quizzes all the time.
3. I love to dance, **but** I will study business in college.
4. Snorks have a snork **and** live under water.
5. She will go to the Institute of Toenail Study, **for** she is destined to do so.

That's it. We're done with simple and complex. Moving along through the woods, we're sure to encounter idioms and slang and split infinitives soon, but not quite yet.

126 . Stuff to Know and Stuff to Avoid

MAKE IT PARALLEL

> Whaaa? Make *what* parallel? What's the matter with you guys? *Parallel* is a *math* term! Are you trying to sneak in some math?

Good grief, no! This author can't add 2 + 2! That's why I do grammar.

Your sentences need to be *parallel*. This seems to be one of the biggest grammar problems for a lot of people, And, like Chi, you may know what parallel means in math class: Two things run in the same direction at the same angle and never meet.

Parallel sentences work much the same way. This means that similar ideas are expressed in similar form, which makes it easier for the reader (or the person who is listening to you) to recognize the similar ideas you are trying to express. When you put words together in a sentence, they need *balance*. In order to do that, you need to treat them the same. For example:

Chi loves grammar, but she is hating math.

Sounds funny, right? But what if you said it like this?

Chi **loves** grammar but **hates** math.

Sounds better, right? Again, using your ear solves many of these grammatical problems. However, if you think about "balance," then the idea is simply to do the same thing on one side that you do to the other. In grammar, that means you use a *parallel* form.

The best way to learn how to create parallel sentences is to learn by the common mistakes people make.

> **My dad says you *learn* from your mistakes. I make a lot of mistakes, so I must be brilliant!**

Exactly. Let's look at the common mistakes people make. There are two ways people most commonly mess up the parallel structure of their sentences: in lists and with correlative conjunctions. (Remember those? *neither-nor, either-or.*) We went over the rules for the correlative conjunctions on page 82, so we'll mostly focus on lists here, with a quick review of the correlative conjunctions.

The other most common mistake occurs with lists. Items in a list should have similar articles. (Remember articles from the last chapter? *a, an, the*)

Incorrect: I put on a hat, the scarf, and a pair of boots.

Here, the *articles* in the list are not the same, so the sentence is not balanced. Make the articles the same and you have balance.

Correct: I put on a hat, **a** scarf, and a pair of boots.

128 . Stuff to Know and Stuff to Avoid

Incorrect: I went in June, July, September, and in December.

Above, we've added an extra word—*in*—after the conjunction *and*. By removing the extra word, below, the sentence becomes balanced.

Correct: I went in June, July, September, and December.

Now, look at these examples:

Incorrect: My grades are better than Sharon.

Correct: My grades are better than Sharon**'s grades.**

What does this have to do with parallel construction? Well, the incorrect sentence is not balanced, so its meaning is unclear. Let's look at it again with explanations:

Incorrect: My grades are better than Sharon.

Here, you're comparing the *grades* to *Sharon herself*—not to Sharon's *grades*.

Correct: My grades are better than Sharon's grades.

Here, by making *Sharon* possessive and adding the word *grades*, we have balanced the first half of the sentence with the second half, and the meaning is much clearer than that of the incorrect sentence.

When you use expressions such as **both/and, neither/nor, not/but,** and **either/or**, make sure your construction is parallel in both parts of the sentence—the part before the conjunctions and the part after the conjunctions.

Incorrect: Neither boys nor the girls like science lab.

Correct: Neither boys nor girls like science lab.

Stuff to Know and Stuff to Avoid . 129

Here, we got rid of the "the" in front of *girls*, so it would be parallel to *boys*.

Incorrect: He was not a green Smurf, but blue.

Correct: He was not a green Smurf, but **a** blue **Smurf.**

Here, we added *a* and *Smurf*, so it would be parallel to *green Smurf*.

Incorrect: She had not two pairs of shoes, but thirty.

Correct: She had not two pairs of shoes, but thirty **pairs.**

Here, we added *pairs*, so it would be parallel to *two pairs*.

Wow! Thirty pairs of shoes would be both a dream come true and the coolest thing ever!

Get Wise!

Put a "C" on the line if the construction of the sentence is parallel. Put an "X" on the line if the construction of the sentence is *not* parallel.

1. _____ His car was so much cooler than Craig.

2. _____ Do you know anything about Madagascar Hissing Cockroaches?

3. _____ "She is too cool for school," is one of my mom's most stupid sayings.

4. _____ Who are buried in Grant's tomb?

5. _____ Either "The Osbornes" or "The Real World" are my favorite show.

How Wise?

1. __x__ His car was so much cooler than **Craig's car.**

2. __c__ Do you know anything about Madagascar Hissing Cockroaches?

3. __c__ "She is too cool for school," is one of my mom's most stupid sayings.

4. __x__ Who **is** buried in Grant's tomb?

5. __x__ Either "The Osbornes" or "The Real World" **is** my favorite show.

132 • Stuff to Know and Stuff to Avoid

HOW TO NOT SPLIT (OOPS!) YOUR INFINITIVES

> **Hmmm...** *Sounds* like infinity: A never-ending process that goes on and on and on...sort of like this grammar lesson!

Okay, we'll ignore that comment, Chi. It *does* sound like that, but once again, the English language is a strange thing, and *infinitives* have nothing at all to do with *infinity*. We won't try to figure out why an infinitive is called an infinitive. All you need to know is how to arrange one. Here's what an infinitive looks like:

to plus a verb:

- ★ to run
- ★ to go
- ★ to bake

We know you've all heard of that huge, common grammatical mistake: *splitting infinitives*. Ow! That sounds like it hurts. So, what the heck is a split infinitive anyway?

It is when you insert a word between the word "to" and the verb. Like we did in the title of this section. We should have said "How not to split your infinitives," instead of "How to not split your infinitives." Let's look at another example:

To boldly go where no woman has ever gone before.

Stuff to Know and Stuff to Avoid . 133

This is incorrect. The verb "to go" is *split* by the word "boldly."

> **And I think *I* will go *boldly* where no woman has ever gone before—outta here!**

Thanks, Chi. Let's go through some more examples:

Incorrect: To quickly run

Correct: To **run quickly**

Incorrect: To sloppily dress

Correct: To **dress sloppily**

You need to get this split infinitive thing right. We guarantee it will show up on a test somewhere. You're sure to encounter it and attempt to use it the wrong way if you don't keep the rule in mind.

134 • Stuff to Know and Stuff to Avoid

Get Wise!

Put a "C" on the line if the infinitive is *not* split. Put an "X" on the line if the infinitive *is* split.

1. _____ It's one thing to happily accept an invitation to a party, but not to happily accept an invitation when you have another party to go to already (even if the second party is better).

2. _____ Do you know how to write a haiku poem?

3. _____ She wants to badly go to the prom with the captain of the football team.

4. _____ To look sadly upon something like that is just wimpy.

5. _____ Don't you know anything? How are you going to do that?

How Wise?

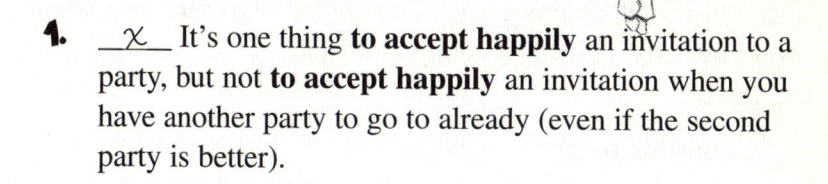

1. __x__ It's one thing **to accept happily** an invitation to a party, but not **to accept happily** an invitation when you have another party to go to already (even if the second party is better).

2. __c__ Do you know how to write a haiku poem?

3. __x__ She wants **badly to go** to the prom with the captain of the football team.

4. __c__ To look sadly upon something like that is just wimpy.

5. __c__ Don't you know anything? How are you going to do that?

136 · Stuff to Know and Stuff to Avoid

DON'T USE NO DOUBLE NEGATIVES

Hey! Finally we get to the subtitle of the book! We hope you recognize that the phrase "don't use no double negatives" is incorrect—since it uses a double negative. The phrase "don't use no" should be "don't use **any**." This is a common mistake, and now you can avoid making it.

A **double negative** is when you use two negative words in a sentence, usually in an effort to make a positive statement. The movie *Can't Hardly Wait* made use of a common double negative. Let's look at the phrase used in a sentence:

Incorrect: I can't hardly wait for spring break.

This sentence technically implies that the speaker does *not* care about spring break!

Correct: I can't wait for spring break.

or

I can hardly wait for spring break.

Both of the correct sentences use only a *single* negative word to express a positive thought. So, if you said:

I can't get no good grades.

You're actually saying:

I can't get—no good—grades.

→ I can get good grades.

Just remember this: In the world of grammar (as in the icky world of math), two negatives equal a positive.

> **So, if two negatives equal a positive, do my two F's in math equal an A?**

Anyway, if you see two negatives in a sentence:

> She don't know nothing

it has to mean the opposite:

> She **does** know something.

So, take one negative out if you see two. Double negatives distort the meaning of the sentence, and they sound absolutely horrible. Don't use them!

138 . Stuff to Know and Stuff to Avoid

AGREEMENT AND HOW TO GET IT

Those crazy subjects and verbs—they often don't agree. And really, you don't want your subjects and verbs to disagree with one another—they can get quite loud when they're having a disagreement, kinda like any couple you can think of (like Peg and Al Bundy).

Subjects must match in number and person (first, second, or third, remember?) to their verbs. It's easy to get confused. But subject/verb agreement is one of the areas where your ear can really help you. Sentences really don't sound right when the subjects and verbs don't agree.

Take a look at this:

> Xavier run for the hills.

Sounds weird, doesn't it? The sentence should read:

> Xavier **runs** for the hills.

Subjects and verbs must **always** agree in person and number. This **never** changes, and there are **no exceptions**—which is nice, since there are so many exceptions in grammar. And do not make this common mistake:

Incorrect: it don't

Correct: it **doesn't**

How will you remember this? You just will. There are no tricks, you just have to remember that "it *don't*" is always wrong. So, if you say it, eliminate it from your vocabulary.

Stuff to Know and Stuff to Avoid . 139

If the subject of the sentence is more than one word, people often get confused, as well—especially if the word that comes right before the verb is plural, as in the following example:

Incorrect: The Queen of Hearts **don't** like Alice.

Here, you need to modify "Queen," which is singular. "Of Hearts" is just a phrase that describes the Queen.

Correct: The Queen of Hearts **doesn't** like Alice.

It is also easy to get confused about subject/verb agreement when *compound subjects* are involved. Compound subjects use the conjunctions *and, or, neither,* and *nor* to connect the subject. Follow these rules:

★ When the compound subject has *either* or *neither*, it's considered *singular.* You can figure this out by separating the subject and seeing what verb it would take.

Neither Josie nor Joe **makes** dinner. (Josie *makes /* Joe *makes*)

Either the principal or the teacher **ruins** everything. (principal *ruins /* teacher *ruins*)

★ And finally, a personal pet-peeve of ours:

Never say "I **seen**." Either say "**I've** seen" or "I **see**." Trust us.

Get Wise!

Put a "C" on the line if the subject and verb agree or an "X" on the line if the subject and verb do *not* agree.

1. _____ She drink water everyday after practice.

2. _____ Neither blue dragons nor green dragons interests him much.

3. _____ She don't know what she's done to him; his heart is broken.

4. _____ Either you or I go to the stupid pep rally.

5. _____ Both Margie and Ellen tries out for the part, although no one else wants it.

How Wise?

1. __x__ She **drinks** water everyday after practice.

2. __x__ Neither blue dragons nor green dragons **interest** him much.

3. __x__ She **doesn't** know what she's done to him; his heart is broken.

4. __c__ Either you or I go to the stupid pep rally.

5. __x__ Both Margie and Ellen **try** out for the part, although no one else wants it.

HOW NOT TO MISPLACE YOUR MODIFIERS

Darn it! Those pesky modifiers are always getting misplaced—we think they go to the same place as all the socks that escape from the dryer. *Modifiers* are adjectives. If you use them in the wrong place in the sentence, they change the meaning of the sentence. (Remember "Word Order" from the previous chapter, or are you losing brain cells at this point?)

You really do have to be careful about where you place your modifiers in a sentence. But here's a clue: your modifiers should be as close to the word they are modifying as possible. Take a look:

Our school had a **bad** book sale.

What's bad, the sale or the books? Maybe both, but that's not really clear from the sentence. Look at this:

Our school had a **sale of bad books.**

Aha! So, it's the *books* that are bad, not the sale. And the reason it is clear now is because the adjective (the modifier) is closer to "books."

Although, one can make the argument that a sale with bad books must be a bad sale.

Stuff to Know and Stuff to Avoid . 143

You don't want the person to whom you are speaking to be confused. Make it clear.

Incorrect: The hot dog was panting.

What's panting—a dog that is hot or a hot dog that you eat?

Correct: The dog was hot and panting.

or

The dog was panting because he was hot.

Has anyone seen my modifiers?

144 . Stuff to Know and Stuff to Avoid

Get Wise!

Rearrange the following sentences so the misplaced modifier is in the correct place. You may have to rewrite a little.

1. I'd like a cold cup of slime.

2. The sign said, "Jeans for her sale."

3. The house is for sale with the dresser.

4. Hold the pickles with my sandwich, please.

5. Move the lawn mower with the rake.

How Wise?

1. <u>I'd like a cup of cold slime.</u> (The way the sentence originally read, the *cup* was cold, not the slime.)
2. <u>The sign said, "Sale on Women's Jeans."</u> (The way the sentence originally read, a reader might think she needs jeans for her own personal sale.)
3. <u>The house is for sale and comes with the dresser.</u> (The way the sentence originally read, the house would be free with the purchase of the dresser—you know that can't be true!)
4. <u>Do not put pickles on my sandwich.</u> (The way the sentence originally read, the sandwich maker would be holding a sandwich in one hand and pickles in the other.)
5. <u>Move the lawn mower and the rake.</u> (The way the sentence originally read, you would make the lawn mower and the rake move at the same time.)

IDIOMS, CLICHÉS, AND SLANG

Idioms

Idioms are phrases or sayings that, when read literally, mean something different from their accepted meaning.

> Idioms? Or do you mean idiots? 'Cause my brother's an idiot. I'd like to learn more about this "idiot" thing so I can insult him when he picks on me.

Sorry, Chi. We're not talking about *idiots,* we're talking about *idioms*, and idioms have nothing to do with idiots.

If you think of idioms as *sayings*, it might be easier. Let's look at some common idioms. As you read them, think how they would sound if you were not a native speaker of English. They would sound either weird or like nonsense.

She's *pigheaded.*

Taken literally, this would mean she had the head of a pig. It actually means "she's stubborn."

I'll grab lunch *on the fly.*

This would literally mean you eat lunch **on** an actual fly, which would be hard since flies are pretty small.

You're the *apple of my eye.*

Huh? Eyes don't have *apples.*

Note that idioms are different from *slang*. Idioms are widely accepted phrases that are acceptable in all kinds of speech. Every language has idioms. In France a few years ago, people would say something was *cowly good* (they'd say it in French, of course) or *cool* in their lingo. What's cool about cows? What the heck does "cowly good" mean? It's weird, we'll admit, but think really hard about the idioms you hear every day—none of them actually make sense when taken literally, like "it ain't over 'til it's over" —huh?— and "bird brain." Who actually has a brain the size of a bird's brain, except a bird?

You should stay away from idioms when you are doing any kind of formal writing in class, like essays. You don't want to lose points because you use an idiom the reader isn't familiar with—that would really stink.

Slang

Ahhh, the part you've been waiting for. *Slang* sounds like a naughty subject, but it's really not, even if some slang words are curses. There are lots of slang words that aren't "dirty." And slang is an interesting topic, if you think about it in terms of language.

Every generation has its own slang words. Think about it. Slang is a way for teenagers to almost "talk in code" around their parents. Every generation of teenagers has its own slang. And slang words can go out of fashion. Think about the slang words your grandparents used:

nifty

jeepers

jalopy

How weird are those words? Who uses them anymore? No one—but hey, they're so "out" maybe they can be "in" again. Have you ever heard the term "in like flynn"? We have, and we used it in high school (which wasn't that long ago for us). But "in like flynn" actually refers to Errol Flynn, an actor from your grandparents' time. So, some slang words do make a comeback.

And, your parents probably used some funny slang words too, like *groovy, chill pill,* and *right on.* Funny sounding words, right? But "right on" has made a comeback, so slang really does work in cycles.

We can't write you a list of all the slang words we know, because the list would be endless. Think about the slang terms you use everyday.

There are some slang terms that we use so commonly today that most adults become confused when they hear them—and isn't that cool?

sweet   This doesn't puzzle adults so much as our next term, but it's puzzling. *Sweet* has to do with taste. Nowadays, it's used to mean cool, as in: "Those kicks are sweet."

sick   This is one of our personal favorites. We all know the literal meaning of *sick,* but now it also means, like, really cool. "That was the *sickest* show I've seen yet." This term is guaranteed to confuse every non-savvy adult you encounter.

We're sure you can think of about a zillion other slang terms you use every day. Keep them out of writing and formal speaking; using slang in those situations would be way uncool.

Try going one day without using any of them. Can you do it? We're skeptical, but go ahead and try. And a gold star for you if you succeed!

150 • Stuff to Know and Stuff to Avoid

Get Wise!

Try the following crossword puzzle of common slang terms. See how you do, and have fun!

ACROSS

2. My friends are my _____

4. I gave her mad _____ for sticking to her own style.

6. It's my fault. (2 words)

8. The info (Spell out this number.)

DOWN

1. Cool, sick

3. You look great! You're totally _____.

4. Goodbye (2 words)

5. Cooler than cool

7. Your date stood you up? What a _____!

Stuff to Know and Stuff to Avoid

HOW WISE?

Across
2. peeps
4. props
6. my bad
8. four one one

Down
1. sweet
3. styling
4. peace out
5. phat
7. bummer

```
            1
            s
            w
   2        3       4        5
   p e e p  s       p r o    p  s
   e        t       e        h
   t     6  m y b   a d      a
            l       c        t
         7  b       e
         8  f o u r o n e    o  n  e
            m       g        u
            m                t
            e
            r
```

152 . Stuff to Know and Stuff to Avoid

Clichés

Clichés are kind of like idioms, but they are **corny and cheesy.** Yes, clichés are things like pickup lines and stupid sayings. You should really avoid clichés, if you can. Clichés are sayings that may have once had meaning or sounded good, but people used them so much throughout time that the words became stale. So, while an expression may have once been a really good tool to help illustrate a point, it now has the opposite effect. We know that sometimes a cliché seems to say the right thing, but you can usually think of a better, more *original* way to say it.

> **Check out this *cliché* pickup line some dweeb just used on me at the mall: "Your daddy must have stolen the stars from the sky and put them in your eyes." I mean, yuck! How cheesy is that?**

Ummm, good one, Chi. That's one of the worst pickup lines out there that we've heard. Here are some more clichés:

> Are you tired? Because you've been running through my dreams all night.

> She's the bee's knees.

(This means she's cool, and it's obviously an oldie.)

> What goes around comes around.

Pleeeassseee...so overused.

Stuff to Know and Stuff to Avoid . 153

Sometimes, people use the word *cliché* to describe a stereotype. You may hear people say something like:

> This may sound **cliché**, but that cheerleader really is peppy.

This is actually a stereotype—cheerleaders are peppy—and not a cliché. But, like idioms, the use of clichés themselves and the word *cliché* has become distorted with common use, so, go ahead and say something is cliché if you want to, but saying its *stereotypical* would be better.

chapter 5

Punctuation Counts

Why is punctuation important; i don't. think it—does any=thing to help my writing be clear?...

Well, Chi's sentence could use a little fixing, since she did not use a single punctuation mark correctly, and it interferes with the meaning of her sentence. Luckily for Chi (and for you), punctuation is easy to

156 . Punctuation Counts

learn. At this point in the book, you've probably had enough of grammar anyway, right? Well, don't despair. This chapter will be quick and *easy*. We've set it up in lists of rules for each punctuation mark. That way, if we can't convince you to read this chapter straight through, you can use it as a reference tool. We split the chapter as follows:

★ Punctuation that ends a sentence:

> **period .**
>
> **question mark ?**
>
> **exclamation point !**

★ Punctuation in the middle:

> **comma ,**
>
> **semicolon ;**
>
> **colon :**
>
> **hyphen - and dashes — , –**
>
> **parentheses ( )**
>
> **quotation marks " "**

So, let's start at the beginning with how to end a sentence!

PERIODS, QUESTION MARKS, AND EXCLAMATION POINTS

Periods

Use a *period* to end a sentence. That's it. Do not use periods to end questions or exclamations. Use periods strictly for **statements** or **commands.** For example:

> I hate my brother's smelly sneakers. (**statement**)

> Throw out those smelly sneakers. (**command**)

Question Marks

Use *question marks* to end sentences that are questions. (Duh!)

> I bet you're waiting for more rules on question marks? That's funny, 'cause there aren't any more. How easy it that?

For example:

> Do you like gummy worms?

> Do you have an X-Box or a Game Cube?

Why in the world would anyone eat something as gross as gummy worms?

Exclamation Points

Use *exclamation points* to end exclamations, which are statements made with excitement or force. A good rule of thumb: **Never** use more than one exclamation point at the end of a statement. The exclamation point already serves to exhibit an intensity of feeling, so it is redundant to include more than one—sort of like saying something is "most perfect" or "totally sanitary." And don't use too many exclamations in your writing, either. A paper littered with exclamation points "shouts" at the reader and often makes the author look scatterbrained. Use them with care! (See, we really didn't need the exclamation point there; we should have used a period. Sorry for "shouting" at you.)

For example:

No way! I can't believe she did that!

Get out! I hate you!

Watch out!

Get Wise!

Place the correct punctuation at the end of the following sentences. Your choices are: period, question mark, and exclamation point.

1. Why do you think those silly girls in horror movies are always wearing nightgowns and doing stupid things____
2. I mean, I'm constantly yelling at the characters____
3. Don't go in there____
4. Then they inevitably get caught by the killer____
5. That is why I hate horror movies____

How Wise?

1. Why do you think those stupid girls in horror movies are always wearing nightgowns and doing stupid things**?**
2. I mean, I'm constantly yelling at the characters**.**
3. Don't go in there**!**
4. Then, they inevitably get caught by the killer**.**
5. That is why I hate horror movies**.**

PUNCTUATION IN THE MIDDLE

Commas

The good 'ol comma is almost always hanging around, you know, in one way or another. That's because the comma can be used in more ways than any other type of punctuation. So, there are quite a few rules as a result. But don't panic! Comma use is not hard, as long as you know the rules (and they are *easy* rules). The following is a list of the rules and examples. (There are more examples given for some of the more involved comma rules.)

> "Who gets *involved* with commas?"

1. Use commas to separate a series of three or more elements. **Always** include a comma before the word *and*. Always. It used to be acceptable to not include it, but nowadays, there is a shift toward putting the comma before *and*—besides, it will only make your sentences more clear.

   > My little sister borrowed my skirt, shoes, and earrings.

   You **don't** need a comma for two things; you can use a conjunction:

   > I like **apples and oranges**.

But, again, for more than two things, use those commas!

Correct: I hate my math, science, and history teachers.

Incorrect: I hate my math, and science teachers.

2. Use commas to separate two *independent clauses* that are connected by a conjunction. Remember, an independent clause is a clause that can also stand on its own as a complete sentence—hence, *independent*.

> Janna is so cool, and she doesn't care what other people think.

This sentence could be broken down into two sentences, so the comma is necessary.

> Janna is so cool.

> She doesn't care what other people think.

Now, if the sentence looked like this:

> Janna is so cool and doesn't care what people think.

"And doesn't care what people think" cannot stand on it's own as a sentence.

> Janna is so cool.

This part is okay as a sentence.

> Doesn't care what people think.

This phrase has no subject, so it can't be a complete sentence.

A cool trick to remember is this rule: If the second clause does not begin with a subject (like "She" in this case), do not use a comma. So, if you can't find a second "he," "she," "Bob," or "Chi," don't use a comma.

Let's look at correct and incorrect examples.

Correct: James coaches soccer every summer, and he loves it.

Incorrect: James coaches soccer every summer, and loves it.

3. Use commas when using introductory words and phrases. The following are some common introductory words and phrases. Remember, these words need commas when they act as "introducers" to the sentence. They may not need commas if they appear in the middle of a sentence.

first

last

finally

in addition

in addition to

most likely

however

consequently

There are many more introductory words—too many to list, but you should get the idea from the preceding list. Let's look at some correct and incorrect examples.

Correct: Finally, the stupid test was over, and I had my license.

Incorrect: She finally, passed the stupid test.

Correct: In addition, she really is not the sharpest tool in the shed.

Correct: In addition to not being the sharpest tool in the shed, she is not very nice.

Incorrect: She is not very nice in addition, to being stupid.

> First, I'd like to dye my hair pink. Then, I can freak out my mom. I can then go to the first punk concert of my life.

4. Use commas to separate non-necessary phrases and interjections (interruptions) from the rest of the sentence. Non-necessary phrases are phrases that can be removed from the sentence, and the sentence will still be complete.

Correct: The house, which is an atrocious shade of green, has been for sale for seven years.

164 . Punctuation Counts

The phrase "which is an atrocious shade of green" is not necessary to the sentence. Without it, the sentence would read, "The house has been for sale for seven years." This is still a complete sentence, so you know you need commas around the phrase, "which is an atrocious shade of green."

Incorrect: The, atrocious shade of green, made the house hard to sell.

You can't put commas around the phrase "atrocious shade of green" here, because without that phrase, the sentence would read, "The made the house hard to sell." That's not a complete sentence, which should tell you not to put commas in.

Correct: I know my teacher takes math seriously, but, gosh, is it boring!

Correct: The girl over there, the one with all the tattoos, is cool.

Incorrect: The, girl with all the tattoos, is cool.

Correct: The girl with all the tattoos, for instance, is cool.

5. Use commas for addresses and dates.

I live at 29 Samson Drive in East Windsor, NJ.

I was born on March 7, 1979.

Punctuation Counts • 165

6. Use commas to set off words or phrases that explain or define a term used in a sentence. We've separated this from non-necessary phrases because these "definitions" could be considered necessary.

Correct: Jim, who broke his wrist playing basketball at home, can't play in the Varsity game this Friday.

The phrase "who broke his wrist playing basketball at home" defines Jim.

Incorrect: Jim, broke his wrist playing basketball at home, and can't play in the Varsity game this Friday.

The phrase "broke his wrist playing basketball at home" describes *what happened* to Jim, but it does not *define* Jim, and it's necessary to the sentence.

7. Use a comma for two adjectives that can also be separated by *and*.

Correct: The smart, sly fox got the food out of the trap without harming himself.

If you didn't use a comma, you'd have to say, "The smart **and** sly fox…"

Correct: The sad, lonely boy found an imaginary friend.

Get Wise! Mastering Grammar Skills www.petersons.com

166 . Punctuation Counts

8. Use commas to separate a statement from a question when they appear in the same sentence.

    Correct: I can leave whenever I want to, right?

    Correct: I can do it, can't I?

9. Use commas to separate *yes, no,* and *names of address* (what you call people when you are speaking to them) from the rest of the sentence.

    Yes, you are a dork.

    No, you may not borrow my favorite sneakers.

    Mr. Brooks, what do you think of my paper?

    You certainly can eat a tadpole, Taylor.

10. Use commas to separate sets of quotes in a sentence or conversation.

    My mom said, "Don't go in there."

    "Your uniform is an absolute mess," the teacher said.

Yay! No more commas!

Get Wise!

Insert commas in the correct places in the following sentences. Refer to the rules if you need to. This is not meant to be a torture test.

> Hmmm . . . torture by punctuation. Sounds scary . . . and *torturous.*

1. Finally Mr. Green gave us our term papers which he's had for a month.
2. Pink purple orange green black and gold are my favorite colors.
3. I was going to the store and… wow look at that guy!
4. Angela was born on May 3 1989.
5. You don't think getting my belly button pierced will hurt do you?
6. "Melanie" my mom said "you're just impossible."
7. Do you think this dress looks okay Mrs. Dunlop?
8. No it won't be necessary to eat a chipmunk.
9. The Cheshire cat grinned for days and days.
10. I think Josh is cute but boy is Adam cuter!

Punctuation Counts

How Wise?

1. Finally, Mr. Green gave us our term papers, which he's had for a month.
2. Pink, purple, orange, green, black, and gold are my favorite colors.
3. I was going to the store and… wow, look at that guy!
4. Angela was born on May 3, 1989.
5. You don't think getting my belly button pierced will hurt, do you?
6. "Melanie," my mom said, "you're just impossible."
7. Do you think this dress looks okay, Mrs. Dunlop?
8. No, it won't be necessary to eat a chipmunk.
9. The Cheshire cat grinned for days and days. (**no comma needed**)
10. I think Josh is cute, but, boy, is Adam cuter!

Semicolons

Semicolons are often misused, especially by adults! In fact, few people get this right. But *you* will master their use because it's simply a matter of knowing there are only three ways to use a semicolon correctly.

1. Semicolons are most often used in place of a conjunction to separate two independent clauses. Should you use a conjunction or a semicolon? Or should you make two sentences? Actually, you get to decide that, as we're going to show you here. You'll have to use your own judgment when deciding if you want to use the semicolon or start a whole new sentence. It's a matter of sound. Remember we told you you'd learn to use your ear? Check it out. Which sounds better to you?

> Jessie laughed when his friend got sick while dissecting the frog; he felt bad about that later. (**use of semicolon**)

> **or**

> Jessie laughed when his friend got sick while dissecting the frog. He felt bad about that later. (**two sentences**)

> **or**

> Jessie laughed when his friend got sick when dissecting the frog, and he felt bad about that later. (**comma and conjunction**)

We think the semicolon works best here because the thoughts are too connected to be two separate sentences. In the same way, using the conjunction "and" makes the sentence too long. What do you think? Each way is correct!

2. Use a semicolon when the second independent clause (in a sentence with two independent clauses) begins with a transitional word, such as *therefore.*

> We will not wait for any latecomers; therefore, get here on time.

Make sure you use a comma after the transitional word that appears after the semicolon.)

3. The third use of semicolons is to separate items in a list that are lists themselves.

> **I've been quiet long enough! What did you just say? I don't think that made sense.**

Chill out Chi, and take a deep breath. It's easier than it sounds. You know you need commas to separate lists of more than two items, but you're separating lists within lists. Look at the examples below to clear things up.

> At the mall, she got shoes, socks, and underwear; notebooks, pens, and pencils; and a really cool jacket.

Remember that if there is **one** part of your list that has multiple items, you still need the semicolon.

> For the salad, you need radishes, tomatoes, and carrots; oil and vinegar; and croutons.

In closing, remember this, please: Many people believe you need a semicolon for lists of single items that follow a colon. This is *not true*. The three uses we listed above are the *only* instances when you can use a semicolon.

Get Wise!

Write a "C" on the line if the semicolon use is correct in the sentence. Write an "X" on the line if the semicolon is not necessary.

1. _____ She grabbed her backpack too quickly; everything spilled out.

2. _____ Henry had to get the following things at the store: hairspray; shampoo; and gel.

3. _____ Barbara needed to get salt, sugar, and cinnamon; as well as apples for her pie.

4. _____ Gabbie went shopping; then she had lunch with her sister at Friday's.

5. _____ The following majors are offered: physical, biological, and earth science; bug studies, animal studies, and fish studies; and English literature.

How Wise?

1. __c__ She grabbed her backpack too quickly; everything spilled out.

2. __x__ Henry had to get the following things at the store: **hairspray, shampoo, and gel.**

3. __x__ Barbara needed to get salt, sugar, and **cinnamon, as** well as apples for her pie.

4. __c__ Gabbie went shopping; then she had lunch with her sister at Friday's.

5. __c__ The following majors are offered: physical, biological, and earth science; bug studies, animal studies, and fish studies; and English literature.

Colons

The colon is another piece of punctuation that actually has only a few correct uses in English, but it is misused in about 100 ways. We're not going to confuse you by going over all of the misuses.

1. Use a colon for greetings and salutations in letters.

   Dear Ms. Thisisthemostboringbooki'veeverread:

2. Use a colon when writing time (as in what the clock says).

   5:00   6:00   7:45

3. Use a colon when writing a memo. (You probably don't write memos now, but you will someday!)

   TO: Mr. Angryboss

   FROM: Mr. Unhappyemployee

4. Use a colon to introduce a (long and boring) list after a complete sentence.

   These are the things you need to bring to camp: shorts, boots, backpack, hiking boots, Walkman, t-shirts, and a good attitude.

5. Use a colon before a complete sentence or group of sentences that is very closely related to the preceding sentence.

174 . Punctuation Counts

Another way to think about this is that the first sentence (the one followed by the colon) is something that needs to be *defined*. The sentence (or sentences) that follow *define* the preceding sentence.

> This is what I have to say: Grammar stinks in every way.

Here, the second sentence is closely related to the first. It *defines* "This is what I have to say."

> Let me tell you what's going on: I have two tests on Friday. Then, I have to study for my SATs, which are on Saturday.

Here, the two sentences that follow the colon *define* "what's going on."

A note on capitalization with colon use: If the material that is introduced by the colon is a complete sentence or if it's a quotation, capitalize the first letter of the first sentence. If a list or an incomplete sentence follows the colon, do not capitalize the first word.

6. Use a colon to introduce a list (another list, yes! Again, you'll encounter lots of these as you grow older!) after using the terms *as follows* or *the following*.

> My thoughts on *The Red Pony* are as follows:
> ★ Worst book ever
> ★ The pony dies in the beginning!

- ★ Made me hate John Steinback
- ★ Once again, WORST book EVER!

7. Use a colon to introduce a long quote (one you would set off on its own line) after a complete sentence.

The clown had a lot to say about her skills:

"I've mastered the art of balloon animals. It was a long and difficult struggle, but I got it done. Balloon animals are the key to my success. I have even expanded away from animals; I now make hats and swords and sheathes for the swords."

176 • Punctuation Counts

Get Wise!

Mark a "C" on the line if the colon use is correct in the sentence. Mark an "X" on the line if the colon use is incorrect.

1. _____ Please bring the following things: snorkel, fins, mask, and wet suit.

2. _____ For the dress rehearsal you need: your script, costume, and makeup.

3. _____ I'll tell you what I'm going to do: I'm going to eat those fried worms.

4. _____ Mrs. Robinson: do you have any beets?

5. _____ Her limo will turn into a pumpkin at 12:00 a.m.

How Wise?

1. _C_ Please bring the following things: snorkel, fins, mask, and wet suit.

2. _X_ For the dress rehearsal you **need your** script, costume, and makeup.

3. _C_ I'll tell you what I'm going to do: I'm going to eat those fried worms.

4. _X_ Mrs. **Robinson, do** you have any beets?

5. _C_ Her limo will turn into a pumpkin at 12:00 a.m.

www.petersons.com   Get Wise! Mastering Grammar Skills

Three Dashes? What, You Thought There Was Only One Kind?

Okay, hyphens and dashes are not the most important thing you'll ever learn about grammar. But you should know how to use them, because the rules are easy, and chances are, you'll encounter a dash or two in your career as a student. (And I, the author, will be honest with you, there was a time when even *I* didn't know there were three kinds of dashes. I thought a hyphen was just a hyphen.)

But alas, there are three kinds:

1. hyphens
2. en dashes
3. em dashes (You may never need to really know this *except* if you work in a publishing house like I do! But, we're going to tell you anyway. Remember, we want you to Get Wise!)

Here's how they work.

Hyphens

1. Hyphens are used to connect two words that "belong together" and to break a word if it wraps to two lines.

    Use a hyphen to connect two spelled-out numbers in a fraction when it is used as an adjective.

    There was a two-thirds majority that voted for Brian as class president.

    but

    Brian won the election with two thirds of the vote.

2. Sometimes, hyphens are used to separate prefixes such as *non-, anti-,* and *ex-* in compound words. But, to tell the truth, you will need to look up words you're unsure about. Most dictionaries have lists of words following the entry for prefixes such as *non-* and *under-* that do not take a hyphen, like *nonconformist* and *underrepresented.* There are very few people, adults and kids alike, who know off the top of their heads if a compound word needs a hyphen or not. We all need to use the dictionary.

3. Hyphens in some words help avoid confusion.

> **re-creation**—to create again—needs a hyphen; otherwise, the word would be **recreation**, which has a totally different meaning

> **re-sign**—to sign again—needs a hyphen also, otherwise the word would be **resign**, which means to quit a job

4. When you use a comma to break a word at the end of a line, you must break the word on a syllable. Once again, if you're unsure of where the syllable breaks are, use your dictionary. A small dot will separate the syllables of the word. Place a hyphen where the dot appears and nowhere else.

    NEVER use a hyphen with an adverb that ends in *ly*, except for the phrase *friendly-sounding.*

    Incorrect: lonely-sounding girl

    Incorrect: gently-flowing stream

Em Dashes

There's no list here, because em dashes only have one use. Em dashes are actually two dashes together --. Your word-processing program may have an em dash in special symbols, which looks like —. Either one is okay to use; they mean the same thing. Use em dashes to set off a part of a sentence *that really needs to be set off*. They are used for "dramatic effect" and can most often be replaced by a more traditional punctuation mark, like commas. But do not use too many em dashes—they can become addictive—they make your writing look scattered—like you have no direction—and they are visually annoying—really annoying—if you get the drift—which we think you do. (See how annoying that was?)

> *Get Wise: Mastering Grammar Skills* is the best book I've ever read—and I've read a lot of books.

You could use a comma here instead of an em dash, but the em dash is more dramatic—if that's the effect you're looking for.

A Word to the Wise

You don't have to commit this stuff to memory. You can always look it up here if you're unsure. But using the dashes correctly will make your writing look polished. And the rules are so easy that once you read them, they'll stick in your mind.

En dashes

En dashes (–) are shorter than em dashes, but longer than hyphens. En dashes have two uses.

1. Use an en dash in a range of numbers (including money).

   I need $20–$30 for lunch money.

   But never use an en dash after a preposition. Spell out the word "to" or "and" in that situation.

   I need between $20 and $30 for the school trip.

   Salary ranges from $32,000 to $33,000 for entry-level candidates.

2. Use an en dash in place of a hyphen in a compound adjective, one element of which consists of two words.

   New York–Paris flight

Ellipses, Parentheses, and Quotation Marks

Hey! We're winding down the punctuation…pretty cool, huh? (As if there's anything cool about punctuation.) But these last three things are really easy, and you probably know a little bit about them already.

Ellipses

An *ellipsis* is three dots …

Ellipses, like em dashes, are often overused.

1. Use an ellipsis to indicate material that has been removed from a quote.

    "She said she was tired…later she said she wasn't tired."

    From the ellipsis in this quote, you would know there was text between "tired" and "later" that has been omitted and replaced by …

2. Use an ellipsis for the beginning of a quote that is not a complete sentence.

    The boy's philosophy on ice cream trucks was that he "…believes they are evil."

    but

    The boy had the following philosophy on ice cream trucks, "I believe they are evil."

3. When ending a sentence with an ellipsis, do not include the period OR do include the period.

Time to explain. There are two schools of thought on this topic—go with whichever one your teacher likes. If you use a period and an ellipsis, the period goes after the ellipsis with a space between them.

She loves me... .

We think the extra period is confusing and not necessary. So, if you don't include a period, just use the ellipsis on its own.

She loves me...

Note: Use ellipses with care, please. When you are editing down quotes, make sure that what you remove and replace with ellipses doesn't change the author's meaning.

Parentheses

1. *Parentheses* are used to set off material that is *parenthetical* (unnecessary). Do not use (yes, you) too many parentheses in your writing (like for school and stuff) or you may (will) suffer (really suffer) the consequences. Too many parenthetical remarks makes your writing look scattered, much like too many em dashes. Use them sparingly. If the information is important enough to write about, consider using commas instead.

> If the information is not important (unnecessary), leave it out.

See? We really didn't need to add the word *unnecessary* there.

2. You can also use parentheses to "define" something.

> The PING putter (golf club) is the best on the market.

Here, we've defined the putter as a golf club.

> The Public Broadcasting System (PBS) sometimes shows live concerts.

Here, we've "defined" the initials for PBS. Once we've done this, we can refer to PBS throughout the rest of our writing, instead of writing out the whole name.

In formal writing, avoid too many parentheses unless you are defining something that really needs defining or citing a source of a quote. In informal writing, use your judgment, but we think it's best to stay away from parentheses whenever possible.

Quotation Marks

Quotation marks give everyone a headache; but, they don't have to. Quotation marks (quotes) set off things that are "spoken." Sometimes (as we just did), quotes are used to "highlight" a certain word. Here are the rules:

1. Use quotation marks to set off a quote (duh!) in text or conversation. When you are quoting someone in text, you must show that in some way. The quotes *only* go around the specific text that is being quoted. Don't include prompts (such as *Mary said,*) in the quotes.

   > Marielle said, "I really hate punctuation. I can't wait to be done with this stupid chapter."

2. Periods and commas at the end of quotes **always** go inside the quotation marks if you are from America. In Britain and other places influenced by British English, the period and comma go outside the quotes in some situations. **That doesn't matter—you always put periods and commas inside quotes.** Besides, the Brits use only one quotation mark, so why listen to them? (Sorry, Great Britain.)

   Question marks and exclamation points can go inside the quotes when they are part of the quoted matter; otherwise, they should be placed outside:

   > Okay, so the question is, "where?"

   > How absurd to call that football player a "wimp"!

3. Most quotes that are in text are introduced by a prompt. Sometimes the prompt follows the quote. In either case, separate the prompt from a quote with a comma.

> The pine tree is one of the oldest kind of trees in New Jersey. Diana Bartlett, a tree expert, says, "Pine trees in New Jersey have been in existence for 500 years, the longest of any cone-bearing tree in New Jersey."

Notice that a comma introduces the quote, and the period at the end is *inside* the quotation mark.

4. What about that single quote ('')? Sometimes, you'll have a quote within a quote. For this, you use *single quotes* within the regular quotation marks.

> "Do you know what she said? She said, 'I hate him.' So I guess she won't go to the prom with you."

186 . Punctuation Counts

Get Wise!

Insert the punctuation mark indicated correctly into the sentences that follow. (The punctuation marks are not necessarily given in the order in which they appear in the sentence.)

1. ["/"/,] She went to the store and said to the shopkeeper Don't you ever have any beets in stock?

2. [( )] Ellen is a pretty girl sure she's not the prettiest girl ever and she's nice.

3. ["/"/…] My teacher said, Peas are nature's perfect vegetable lots of vitamins in peas.

4. [( )] The Glee Club GC is in a national competition.

5. [()/ "/"] This is what she said she's so mean, I hate that girl and everything about her!

How Wise?

1. She went to the store and said to the shopkeeper, "Don't you ever have any beets in stock?"

2. Ellen is a pretty girl (sure she's not the prettiest girl ever) and she's nice.

3. My teacher said, "Peas are nature's perfect vegetable… lots of vitamins in peas."

4. The Glee Club (GC) is in a national competition.

5. This is what she said (she's so mean), "I hate that girl and everything about her!"

appendix a

The Biggest (and Most Common) Mistakes and How to Avoid Them

You've made it all the way to the Appendix. Congratulations! It's kind of like your graduation from our crazy school of grammar. And, if you've made it up to here and you've gone through all the exercises with our trusty sidekick, Chi, we can bet you'll be doing a *lot* better on any quiz, test, final, whatever, that may come up. But we're not quite done yet. We want to make sure you are completely equipped with all you need to know to go on your merry way through the rest of high school scoring really high points on the grammar end of things. So, we're giving you a little reference book—something to hang on

190 . Appendix A

to so you have it when you need it. We realized there are some other very common errors that you should know about. And this list will make them easy to access—so try to learn to recognize the error, because you can always look up the "cure" here in this Appendix.

The following list contains common grammatical errors, some of which we may not have discussed and many of which we have. Again, this is your quick reference guide to errors. Think of it as your personal arsenal to combat bad grammar. These mistakes are so common, you're bound to hear people make them every day. Go ahead—be obnoxious and correct them! You deserve it. We didn't teach you all this grammar for nothing! And annoying adults by correcting *their* grammar is almost as good (if not better) than acing a grammar test!

Many of the items involve word confusion. When the following words are used incorrectly, they can drastically alter the meaning of a sentence.

affect / effect

This confuses oh so many people. **Affect** means to *influence* something.

> The fashion on the runways **affects** the fashions in lower price stores.

Effect is the *result* of something.

> The fashion shown on the runways has an inspiring **effect** on me.

Something **affects** you, so you are **effected** by it.

accept / except

Another thing people get confused about. **Accept** means *to approve of, to welcome*.

> When I was finally *accepted* by the cool kids, I realized they were idiots.

Get Wise! Mastering Grammar Skills   www.petersons.com

Except means the same thing as *but*.

> I would have been happy to have finally been *accepted* by the cool kids, *except* I realized they are idiots.

sympathy / empathy

This is a personal pet-peeve of ours. To have **sympathy** for someone means to feel bad about their situation, which *you have never experienced.*

> I have **sympathy** for the starving children of the world.

To experience **empathy** means you feel bad about someone's situation, and you *have experienced the same thing.*

> I really **empathize** with Emily; I swallowed a bug once, too.

its / it's

This one really annoys us (as well as every teacher on Earth.) But it's easy to remember. *Only use it's when you mean "it is."* There is no other time when you need an apostrophe in "its." Even when *its* is possessive, it still gets no apostrophe. *It's* is only correct when you are saying *it is*. We can't seem to say this enough, as we keep repeating ourselves.

they

Lots of people seem to forget that *they* is a plural pronoun and will mix it with a singular noun or pronoun in a sentence.

> *Someone* started a nasty rumor about Amy, and then *they* started one about Sara.

This is incorrect. *They* is plural and *someone* is singular. In this kind of sentence, you must use *he* or *she*, not *they*. If you don't know the gender of the "someone," choose either *he* or *she* or use *he/she* if you must.

Get Wise! Mastering Grammar Skills — www.petersons.com

there / their / they're

Tricky, huh? NO. Easy. Use *there* for location.

> The party is over **there**.

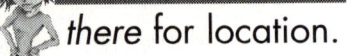

They're is a *contraction* of the words *they* and *are*. Only use *they're* if you mean *they are*.

> **They're** playing Hungry Hungry Hippos.

Their is a pronoun, and it is the *possessive* form of *they*. Only use it when referring to something that *belongs to "them."*

> **Their** dog is adorable.

The dog *belongs* to them.

and / as well as

These are not interchangeable. They have different meanings and should be treated that way! *And* is used to connect two things *of equal importance*.

> being a cheerleader **and** dating the captain of the football team

Use *as well as* to connect two things where the second thing is of *less importance.*

> being a cheerleader is important *as well as* dating the captain of the football team

Here, dating the captain of the football team is important, but not so important as being a cheerleader.

imply / infer

Something is *implied.* Someone *infers.* That is, you can say something that *implies* something to someone, and he or she *infers* what you mean.

> I **implied** that Shelly is not my favorite person. Angela somehow **inferred** from this that I absolutely hate Shelly.

to / two/ too

Most, but not all, people use *two* correctly; that is, for the number 2. But *to* and *too* cause a lot of problems.

To is a preposition. Use it that way. So:

> I went **to** the pep rally.

Too means *also*. Do not use it for location. And don't use it at the beginning of a sentence. You will traditionally see *too* at the end of a sentence—don't forget the comma before *too*.

I went **to** the pep rally, and Janna had to go, **too**.

appendix b

Get Wise! Games

Here are a few puzzles and ad-libs to Get Wise!

PUZZLE ONE: THOSE CONFUSING WORDS

Clue: Look for these words in Appendix A.

Note: You can use apostrophes in this puzzle.

ACROSS

2. What other people think has no _____ on me.
3. Every clique has _____ own style.
4. Emily _____ Amy are best friends.
5. I cannot _____ your invitation to the prom, someone cooler asked me.
7. _____ going to ruin my party if they come.
9. Can I go _____?
10. Kids want to make _____ own decisions about life.
11. I'll hang out with anyone _____ my parents!

DOWN

1. _____ ridiculous to expect us to wear uniforms in school.
3. What did she _____ when she said that about me?
4. Some girls think they can _____ the way everyone thinks, just because they are cool.
5. Pets need lots of love and attention _____ well as food and water.
6. Well, I can _____ that she thinks you're mean.
7. There are _____ things I hate: rain and humidity.
8. The girl over _____ is too cool for this place.
12. I go _____ football practice every day during the season.

ANSWERS

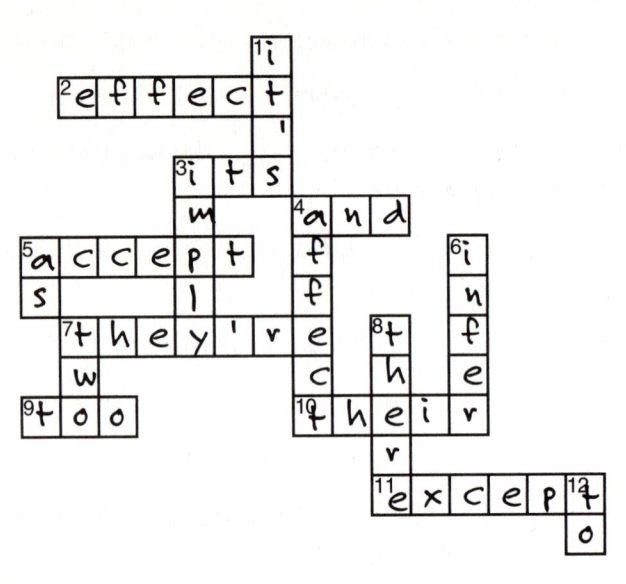

```
         ¹i
   ²e f f e c t
         ³i t s
         m    ⁴a n d
  ⁵a c c e p t f     ⁶i
   s       l  f     n
      ⁷t h e y ' r e  ⁸t  f
      w          c   h   e
  ⁹t o o       ¹⁰t h e i r
                 r
              ¹¹e x c e p ¹²t
                         o
```

Across

2. effect
3. its
4. and
5. accept
7. they're
9. too
10. their
11. except

Down

1. it's
3. imply
4. affect
5. as
6. infer
7. two
8. there
12. to

PUZZLE TWO: GOT WISE!

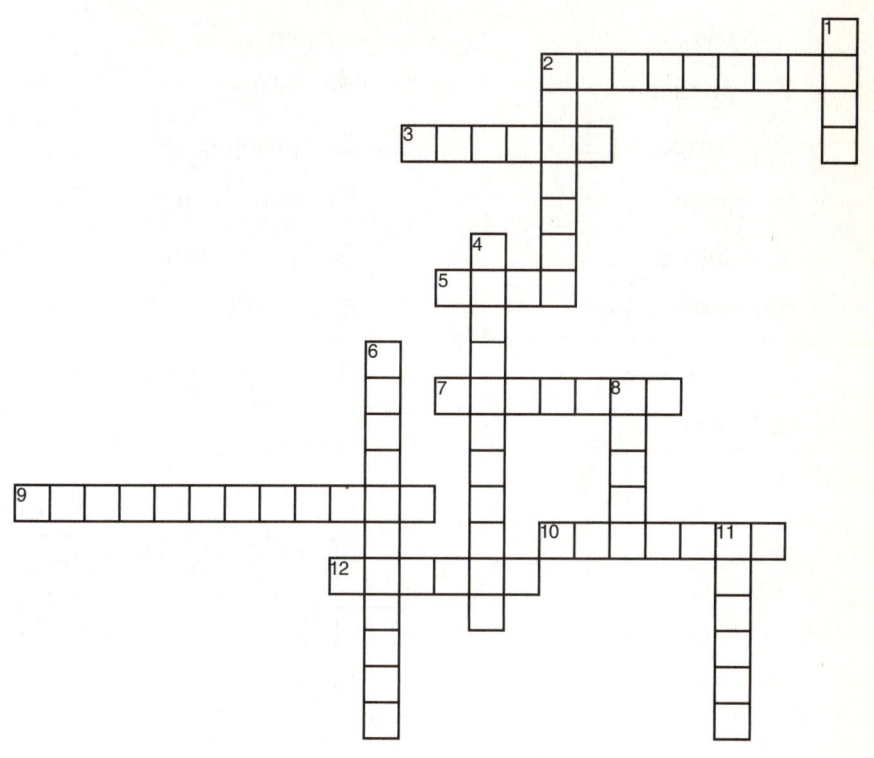

ACROSS

2. Pants
3. At the end
5. A person, place, or thing
7. Shirt
9. Hey!
10. Your new favorite subject in school
12. Chi's name means _____.

DOWN

1. Word of action
2. Takes the place of
4. I join things together
6. Don't end a sentence with a _____.
8. I signal a pause.
11. A friend to words of action

ANSWERS

Across

2. predicate
3. period
5. noun
7. subject
9. interjection
10. grammar
12. wisdom

Down

1. verb
2. pronoun
4. conjunction
6. preposition
8. commas
11. adverb

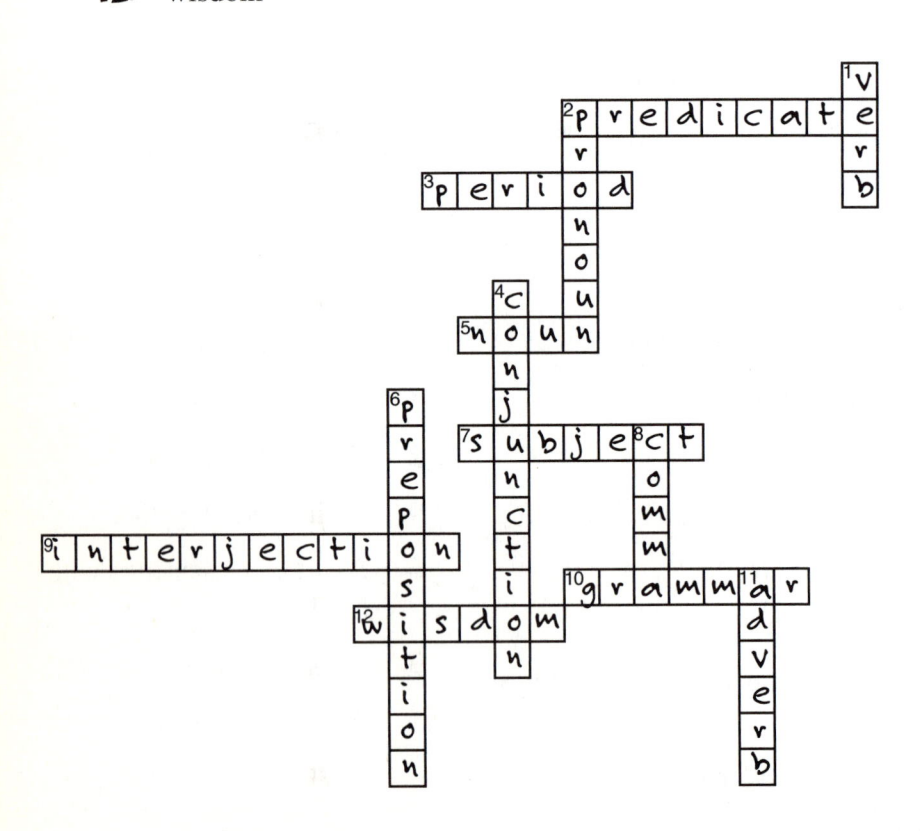

Appendix B • 203

GET WISE FIND!

Words can be up and down, diagonal, forward, and backward.

```
S V A K W N R G D F T M P I X M W E K N
E E X W L M U L E E C N D E I F V P N U
V U V B S X O T W S S I E S R I Y O O M
I V E I E O M C I E O C P M T S L K L B
T C Y Y T T A Q V M B L R C E O O L O E
C U B G C A L C S N A D N I C T V N C R
E W J G W D G A K C M U I I P G A G N U
J A R E Q X R E E E J I M G A T C T Y I
D N M I E X A D N B M E D X P U I D S N
A J B M H I M X U E S D C X L F Y V H F
U A O V O F M S O M L L N S E J A N E I
C R Z G L C A M H H S B V H P V K A H N
K Z M J F V R I V Z H V U A L V W I M I
E M S V W K G B R Y Z L R O T G P J I T
M O D I F I E R N E W P V V D F H A V I
O J O B E L Y T S L F Z H R A E B P R V
C S I R W L H A L S T E V Q Y C H I X E
X A H Y Y N C V A T N C T A G N A H T I
W W R W O C O W Z E T A G U J N O C W G
A B E X C L A M A T I O N K R Z V G Q M
```

ADJECTIVE
CASE
CHI
COLON
COMMA
CONJUGATE
DESCRIPTIVE
DOUBLE NEGATIVES
EXCLAMATION
GRAMMAR GLAMOUR

IDIOMS
INFINITIVE
MISPLACED
MODIFIER
NUMBER
PERSON
SEMICOLON
STATEMENT
STYLE
SUBJUNCTIVE

Get Wise! Mastering Grammar Skills   www.petersons.com

204 • Appendix B

```
S V A K W N R G D F T M P I X M W E K N
E E X W L M U L E E C N D E I F V P N U
V U V B S X O T W S S I E S R I Y O O M
I V E I E O M C I E O C P M T S L K L B
T C Y Y T T A Q V M B L R C E O L O E
C U B G C A L C S N A D N I C T V N C R
E W J G W D G A K C M U I I P G A G N U
J A R E Q X R E E E J I M G A T C T Y I
D N M I E X A D N B M E D X P U I D S N
A J B M H I M X U E S D C X L F Y V H F
U A O V O F M S O M L L N S E J A N E I
C R Z G L C A M H H S B V H P V K A H N
K Z M J F V R I V Z H V U A L V W I M I
E M S V W K G B R Y Z L R O T G P J I T
M O D I F I E R N E W P V V D F H A V I
O J O B E L Y T S L F Z H R A E B P R V
C S I R W L H A L S T E V Q Y C H I X E
X A H Y Y N C V A T N C T A G N A H T I
W W R W O C O W Z E T A G U J N O C W G
A B E X C L A M A T I O N K R Z V G Q M
```

WISE LIB

If you are doing this by yourself, write down on a separate sheet of paper any examples of the following parts of speech in the order they are listed below. Don't peek at the passage on the next page until you're done. Then, turn the page and insert your words into the passage and see the wacky results! (If you are doing this with a friend, simply turn to the passage on the next page, read out the type of word needed for each blank, fill in your friend's words, and check out the results.)

Note: This ad-lib works best with past-tense verbs.

1. adjective
2. noun
3. noun
4. verb
5. noun
6. verb
7. verb
8. noun
9. preposition
10. noun
11. noun
12. verb
13. noun

Appendix B

On top of a _____ _____ ,
              ADJECTIVE   NOUN

All covered with _____ ,
                   NOUN

I _____ my poor _____
   VERB   NOUN

When somebody _____ .
                  VERB

It _____ off the _____
   VERB   NOUN

And _____ to the _____ ,
    PREPOSITION   NOUN

And then my poor _____
                    NOUN

_____ right out the _____
  VERB   NOUN

Turn the page to see Chi's answers.